AF480446

SVARAJ

STRIVE VISUALIZE ACHIEVE

ANURAG MANGLIK

Published by "The Great Indian Book Tour"
Imprint : **Holistic Publishing**
www.tgibt.com
106/91, Ashok marg, Vijay path
Mansarover, Jaipur, Rajasthan-302020
Phone : +91-72400-68114
email : prashant@tgibt.com

Title : **SVARAJ** (STRIVE VISUALIZE ACHIEVE)

Author : **Anurag Manglik**

Copyright © **Anurag Manglik** 2023
All rights reserved

First published in 2023
First Edition 2023
Printed in India
Printer : Manipal Technologies
ISBN : 978-93-93262-21-9
Price : INR 275

This is a work of fiction. Names, characters, places and incidents are part of Author's imagination and resemblance to any actual person, living or dead, events or place is purely coincidental.

All rights reserved. No part of this book can be used, reproduced in any manner whatsoever without written permission from the author, except in the case of brief quotations embodied in articles or reviews.

ACKNOWLEDGEMENT

This book is dedicated to the wonderful woman with whom I am blessed to share my life, to my wife Dr. Anuradha Manglik.

My daughters Dr. Himani and Miss Salloni, pursuing MBBS, deserve special mention for being meticulous and becoming capable individuals.

I would not be what I am today without support of my Parents, who have bestowed unlimited, unconditional love on me to grow with Freedom.

My heartfelt gratitude to my Mentors, for their guidance during very initial stage of my professional career, which became a strong foundation.

My gratitude to my friends and relatives for accepting me as I am and for all love and affection.

Finally, I would like to thank Soka Gakai members and seniors in faith for an amazing spiritual journey without which this book would not have been possible.

PREFACE

We all strive in life to be Happy- and to be Peaceful

The goal in life to be Happy; changes from time to time, for school student it is about getting good grades and making their parents proud, for college student it is about getting good placement, for youth in corporate it is about good salary and good position, for CEO in organization is about achieving performance driven work culture and so on.

Raj was a happy go lucky person in school and college, however his life changed as he entered the corporate world. He was influenced by his mentors in corporate and got enormous support from wife and parents. He realized that only he knew his life, his professional and personal struggles. He didn't have to prove anything to anyone.

He defined his life, a complete Elephant fully aware of partial perspectives of the world around.

This book is about Raj. He understood the importance of parable taught in school "Five blind men and an Elephant". He realized that many a times he himself was blinded by partial perspectives.

This book narrates how Raj found meaning of life in different situations. He molded his life into epitome of Complete picture, Success, and his Freedom.

Contents

1. The Speech : *Sail is Set*   1

2. Those Early Days : *Sailing Instructor*   5

3. First Inspiration : *Happy Sailing*   9

4. Those Golden Days : *Sailing in Free Wind*   15

5. Entering the Door of Corporate : *Sail Started in Ocean*   24

6. Introspection : *Sailor Lost in Ocean*   31

7. Aha Moment : *Learning to Adjust the Sail*   35

8. Living the Holistic Approach : *Setting the Sail – New Destination*   43

9. Life at Its Best : *Sailing Far Wind with strong Helm*   47

10. Sweet Taste of Success : *Sweet Sailing*   56

11. Visulaise "The Elephant" : *Sailor is the Artist where Wind is the Medium*   62

12. Lost Vison in dark clouds : *Sail hitting the storm*   70

13. The Family Hold on : *In Mercy rough waters*   77

14. Sunrays Gleaming though clouds : *Hoisting the Sail*   87

15. Persevering on : *Family that Sails together stays together*   94

16. Homeland : *In need of Star point for setting the sail*   103

17. Challenging Decision : *Adjusting the Sail*   110

18. A Complete Elephant : *All set to Sail for Freedom*   123

19. Freedom : *My Sailboat- My Life- My Rule*   129

20. The Retirement Speech (Continued) : *Sail is Set*   139

1. The Speech

Sail is Set

With a confident and steady stride, Raj headed towards the stage to give his retirement speech. Crossing his wife and daughters seated in the first row, he gave one fleeting glance towards their beautiful faces. His heart swelled with love as they raised their camera and snapped a picture of him, capturing the moment forever.

Raj gave a brief expressionless nod as he continued his way to the podium. He found all eyes at him on the stage. He was surprised at how calm and comfortable he felt. He was neither nervous nor emotional, just completely prepared.

A wide smile spread across his face as he approached the microphone. Today is the day, he thought to himself. Let's do this! Hands planted on his hips: "Special day" Raj said, flashing a beaming white smile. With a tone of incredible gratitude, he continued, "Folks, I am truly blessed to have all of you here. It's such an unique opportunity to express my heartfelt thanks to all wonderful people whom I have worked with, who have helped me get here, and have helped me stay here." The audience cheered for him.

"There is something I want to share with you," said Raj, and his eyes moistened. A long sigh, shuddered from deep inside him, as he stared down at floor. His voice grew faint, the hint of a whisper, "I'm usually not the one for public display of emotions, but today I have permitted myself to just let them flow." He looked down and paused for three seconds as if attempting to gather his thoughts. And then said "I am privileged to live this life alongside a wife like Radha, without whose contribution, my life is incomplete. There were moments when I had given up; it was she who walked with me to provide me with the support that I needed." Raj looked earnestly at his wife. "Radha, today my life is successful, all because of your relentless effort and faith in me. And most importantly, I would like to thank you for giving me our two lovely daughters who have made my life a small paradise here on earth." He glanced at his family for a fraction of a moment and nodded in silent agreement. "Also, I would like to shower my gratitude to my parents for guiding me and doing everything possible to help me succeed."

Shifting his gaze to his colleagues, Raj took a deep breath. One deep breath wasn't enough, so he took a long second one. "Last thing I must do today is share the completeness of my life. You will be surprised to know that I was not very ambitious back in school and college. In fact, most knew me as a happy-go-lucky and unambitious soul. I was a good student, but not the best. I was least concerned about getting good grades. I went to a good college, but not the best or most sought-after colleges in India. I got a good campus placement, but not the best."

"If there has been one thing that I've learned in my life, it is that success does not always mean having a great career, a lot of money, and social recognition. It means achieving specific goals that lead you to your vision of a good life that you have planned for yourself. If you are looking for the key to success, you must set goals and accomplish them."

Raj continued in a soft but assertive tone, I understood

the parable of 'Blind men and the Elephant' very well. "The anecdote that you and I have heard, goes like this. Five blind men were walking along the road when they came across an elephant. They had never been talked about an elephant before, neither had the concept of an elephant been ever communicated to them."

"So, they gathered around this animal and each of them grabbed a different part of the beast. Then they argued about what they'd seen. One blind man felt the elephant's ear and said he'd found a large leaf from a palm tree—he said Elephant is like FAN. The second blind man had the tail – he said Elephant is like a ROPE. The third had the elephant's trunk and said he'd found a hose – he said Elephant is like a PIPE. The fourth ran his hands over one of the elephant's legs and - he said Elephant is like a PILLAR' And the fifth ran his hands over elephant's stomach and - he said Elephant is like a WALL. Each of the blind man had partial and different perspectives of Elephant."

"Once upon a time, even I was influenced by the partial perspectives of society and had defined my Elephant with professional goals only. Later with the help of Radha I could define my complete Elephant which include, Professional, Personal/Family, Health, Finance, Social ties, and spiritual values along with emotions and compassion."

And Raj continued to speak of his success in the face of challenges, "As I stand before you, I can proudly say that I am successful. I am successful because I defined my Elephant, I put little goals for myself, told myself that these targets are important to me, and made a commitment to myself to achieve them. I worked hard and the universe supported me to succeed.

I found the beauty of success in less glamorous things. Today, I enjoy my non-ambitious well-defined lifestyle." Raj said with a smile, as he continued his speech through the detonation of applause.

And in a flash, he remembered his whole life vividly.

2. Those Early Days

Sailing Instructor

"Pay attention to your studies," Raj's father glared down at his son, snapping at him. "This is what will get you through, so just concentrate on your studies." Raj looked up and watched through narrowed eyes as his father exhaled loudly through his nose. He bit down his lip as the pulse shot through his body. He quivered but did not say anything. He twitched a little and his head slumped. He fixed his eyes on the wall before him. He knew he had broken his father's hopes.

"Please, relax!" Raj's mother said in soft voice, lovingly giving her finger to the child. "He will learn."

"Learn when? When will he understand the importance of studies?" his father grumbled.

"When will he learn to think of studying instead of playing the entire day? And when will you stop protecting him and covering up all his mistakes?" he grunted.

She didn't react, but Raj did. Tears started rolling down his cheeks. He stood upright and fixed his eyes on the wall once more, his face as blank as when they'd started. Not even a hint of emotion.

*

Raj had spent much of his early childhood in Ahmedabad. He was a happy-go-lucky boy who lived like a wild and free child—climbing trees, playing football in his neighbourhood park, and other games such as cricket, and marbles. In Raj's life there was one activity that held most importance: spending large amount of his time in play.

Raj's father—like any father—wanted him to acquire a good education. His understanding was that studies were the key to success. Time and again he had warned Raj to focus more on his studies instead of wasting time on playing with friends.

"Just concentrate on your study. That's your only job," his father often said.

But this was the last thing that appealed to Raj. His aim was different. He liked school well enough and was an average student. He made enough grades in most of his subjects. He didn't care much for studies, except science and maths.

As years went by, he improved just enough to avoid failing in any class. The other boys in his class became more and more competitive. Of course, that didn't bother him. He had already detached himself from the expectations of his family and teachers. By the time he was in the seventh grade, his only aim was finishing primary school and seeking admission in a good school.

The older he got, the less value he put on studying and the less time he spent with books. "What do I want in my life?" Raj often wondered. The sad part was that he had no clue.

When people asked Raj about his grades, he relied on the standard statement, "I'm not the studious type." While in his heart he reaffirmed himself, "Who has the time for studying books, when the real work is playing and enjoying?"

He knew that good grades could not define him. So, he continued to study just to survive in the academic system and keep his father happy.

*

A mechanical engineer by profession, Raj's father worked in Space Application Centre, ISRO till the age of 60. Post retirement, he worked in an Engineering College and finally retired at the age of 76, as a professor. He was a self-made man who lived a simple life. He had built an asset base right from scratch, by virtue of his hard work, economical lifestyle, and wise investments. He was satisfied with bare minimum comforts and avoided all nonessential luxuries and material things. Nevertheless, he had made available all the necessities required by his children. He was not a miser, but he believed in saving money. When it came to saving money, no one could beat his dad, not even the finance minister.

He used to travel on a bicycle and preferred eating at home instead of restaurants. He practised in his personal life the aphorism, "Money saved is money earned". He possessed a wristwatch which was gifted, which he had retained all his life.

He used to have an antique radio at home which he was unwilling to change even though better models were available in the market later. Even when the TV started relaying cricket matches, he would watch cricket on the television with the volume turned down and the radio turned up. Raj and his sister used to often taunt him at turning down the live telecast on television and turning up the radio. His answer used to be, "TV commentary isn't descriptive enough." Sometimes the action on the screen was out of sync with the commentary on radio, but no matter, he persisted.

Raj loved his mother. She was all of what a mother should be. She was warm when she hugged him. She was always sweet, gentle and kind. She was one person on whom Raj could count on to be right there beside him when he would get into trouble. She would always take her son's side and save him from the scolding of his father for not studying. Silence was her way of dealing with conflicts and pressures. All these had become a part of Raj's childhood memories.

A spiritual person by nature, she had played a big role in moulding Raj's personality to lead a simple and contented life amidst pressures, challenges, temptations, distractions and scarcities. Thus, the foundations of ethical behaviours were laid down at home in the early formative years by Raj's parents.

3. First Inspiration

Happy Sailing

Diwali vacation had begun, and Raj and his family were on their way to their ancestral home in Vadodara to meet his grandfather, Raj remembered his grandfather as a man of few words, who had led his life based on the principle of 'simple living and high thinking'.

Since childhood, Raj had spent his Diwali holidays at his grandfather's place. He was very happy to celebrate the festival with his uncles, aunts and cousins.

Raj's father had 4 brothers and 3 sisters and every year they would make it a point to meet up at their paternal house. Diwali was still a few days away. But there was a lot of preparation to do.

Raj couldn't wait to start the festive celebrations. Diwali meant meeting all his chachas, chachis and cousins. Diwali meant making marigold garlands and colourful rangolis to adorn the courtyard, each cousin then trying to outdo the other. Everyone would cook together, eat together, and have innumerable chai sessions together. It was a pleasure to watch the entire family sitting together. For him the festival meant, spending the evening curled up around his grandfather (Baba), in a bed that was called takat, listening to the stories from his younger days. Diwali meant wearing new clothes, lighting diya's and bursting crackers with the whole family. The most important thing that Diwali meant for Raj was watching the making of flowerpots (anars) by his family.

*

"Come on Raj," Baba called, "Come and watch us make the anars to adorn the house."

"Yes…of. Yes…!!" chirped Raj, as he followed his grandfather to the courtyard, where all the men of the house had gathered.

Raj's family had a very special tradition of making flowerpots (Anar), the most popular Diwali firecrackers. The family had masterfully crafted the formula of making anars. Each family member knew the exact ratio of the chemicals that needed to be mixed.

All the family members sat flat on the ground in a straight row, with their feet folded under them. Before each one of them lay a neatly folded newspaper. Raj gazed in absolute astonishment as he saw how the house had turned into a small-scale fireworks factory.

All his chachas waited patiently, as Baba inspected the heap of earthen pot shells received from the potter.

Then came the order, which they all waited for, "Let's start the show," ordered Baba, as he smiled approvingly at the empty pots.

One by one, each member of the family started filling the pots with chemical components. Raj watched in awe as his elder chacha filled sulphur in the pot and passed it to the next member who filled the pot with aluminium chips and passed it to the next member. The next member added sulphur, and the next added potassium. Finally, when all the ingredients were added, the filled pots landed with Baba who then sealed the pots.

"Okay, now let's test these five flowerpots." They decided that someone would need to watch the timing of the firework. Raj?" his grandfather asked, "Are you ready to be the time-keeper?"

"Yeah Baba, I am ready," Raj grinned excitedly. He felt a sense of responsibility in being a part of this wonderful process.

"On your mark, get set, go!" The whole family counted as Baba bent down to ignite the anar. As soon as the firework set off, the entire family watched the sparkle of a dazzling array of colours with a sentiment of love and happiness associated with the making of the anar.

As the anar shot dazzling sparkles of colours in the air, everyone sat upright watching intently. It looked every inch the engineering marvel to see the colourful light sparkling among the leaves of the mango trees and the plants in the courtyard.

Everyone waited with bated breath to see how long it would last. As Raj glanced at the watch from time to time, he felt that his heartbeat had gone up.

"Come on! come on! Keep going!! 5 seconds more to go," Baba urged, as showers of coloured sparks spread out from a small pot.

Raj stared at his family's passionate display of emotions for a few moments, then gave a low giggle.

Everyone's expressions changed as the anar started to come to an end. "Oh, no. No, no, no.." said one of Raj's chacha frantically, clutching the arm of his younger brother.

"53 seconds." Said Raj with a sigh. He saw everyone's jaw drop.

Baba was very quiet now. He leaned back and watched the burnt anar intently. He closed his eyes momentarily as if in deep contemplation of the error. Then he spoke and his words were very demanding "Improvise it and bring it to 60 seconds," he said.

"The height was fine, but the colour is not up to the mark." Grumbled one of Raj's Chacha. "I think the blue colour was missing."

""Do you really think so? It looked fine to me," said another.

"No! it wasn't!" the youngest Chacha retorted.

Another Chacha nodded his head vigorously.

Everyone put their heads together and reviewed and discussed ideas how to make the anar last for 60 seconds. They decided to modify the quantity of chemical composition in the pot and retest.

"I think you're right," Baba finally said, pondering. And then continued in his soft, mesmerising tone. "Let's add some more quantity of copper and watch the colours this time."

Taking a deep breath, Baba said, "Okay, my boys…time to get back to work. Let us modify the formula."

"Yes," said everyone in tandem and started making the necessary modifications. After a brief interval, Baba ignited the new anar. Again, the family stared unblinkingly at the sparkling tree as a bunch of stunning colours shot upwards.

Baba raised his eyebrows questioningly. "Raj, how long?"

Raj's upturned face beamed radiantly as he said, "Baba, we

have now achieved 60 seconds!"

Baba's wrinkled old face lighted up with immense joy as he said, "Really!" His cheeks started to glow. It seemed like a moment of personal triumph.

In that instant, there was a spontaneous expression of victory that no words could explain. It was as if they had found some hidden treasure.

For nearly five minutes, the family clapped with intense delight. They laughed, hooted, and cheered enthusiastically.

"Good work, boys," Baba acknowledged admiringly. After that it was time for the family to enjoy the hand-crafted anar.

Raj stared in open awe at those around him. Diwali celebrations taught Raj to cherish the gift of togetherness. These days of togetherness had brought the concept in Raj, that happiness comes with happiness of all people around you. Happiness of accomplishing the target as was anars timings of 60 secs here.

*

Raj's grandfather was a white-haired man. Deep lines around his mouth, showing his age and wisdom that came with it. He had kind-looking blue eyes tucked away behind thick glasses. His face showed strength much like his body. Even though he was in his late seventies, he was still physically and mentally active, managing his chores on his own.

He was a man of independent temperament who believed that his children were his only assets. Uppermost in his mind was the preservation of his family's honour and prestige.

Raj adored his grandfather, and in some ways, he also admired him. He enjoyed the time spent with his Baba and would listen with rapt attention to his practical advice. His young mind was deeply impressed with his Baba's anecdotes of life's hardships, and sufferings, and his patience and perseverance. Baba often told him about how enormously patient his grandmother was and how she brought up all her children with minimum resources.

Raj would ask unending questions to Baba, who patiently and thoughtfully answered them all.

"Baba, you have so little, still you are always happy?" asked Raj. A few minutes passed, and Baba had still not answered the question. He seemed to be caught in memories, sitting in what looked like a trance. Raj looked at him in bewilderment. He had asked a simple question. He did not intrude and waited for him to answer.

"Inner peace," he simply replied after a while. After a brief pause, he then said, "Inner peace is more important than all the riches put together."

Raj didn't think he understood. He raised his eyes and looked at his grandfather. Then he scratched his head with his hand and asked hesitatingly, "What?"

Baba looked at him and smiled.

*

Baba led a simple, self-sufficient lifestyle. He was a practical, down-to-earth man. He had a beautiful heart and was always driven by the desire to help people.

The main thing that impressed Raj was the way he lived his life-not full of greed, but willing to help people-and ready to give his last cent even when he did not have one. He led an honest life regardless of obstacles. And Raj adored him throughout learning from him in his teenage years.

4. Those Golden Days

Sailing in Free Wind

Raj sat in the last row of Section D in Engineering College, with a faraway look in his eyes. He listened with half ear to the orientation program for which the first-year students were seated there.

He glanced at his watch and sighed to himself. "Oh God! Why do these programs have to be so lengthy and boring." he mumbled. His stomach had already started to grumble.

He gazed around looking distinctively bored and uninterested. He shrugged his shoulders and let out a big yawn.

"Good morning, students, and please allow me to introduce myself!" a voice came from the podium grabbing his attention.

"I am, your Engineering Design Professor." She had smoky-grey hair, and her face was serious and expressionless.

"Every year, I set aside some time for the newer students and meet with them to learn about their hobbies and interests outside of the college."

"Ok. I now have something for you that will perhaps lift your spirits a little." the Professor said, and walked to the front row. The students looked eagerly in anticipation.

The Professor looked out over all her students. Her eyes caught a student in the upper-left side of her classroom.

"So, what are your hobbies?" she questioned the student, as she sneakily looked at the floor beneath her desk.

"Madam, my hobbies are playing musical instruments." said the student.

In the mid of his saying, the Professor's eyes scanned all the students. Her eyes met with Raj. Both looked into each other's eyes. The direct eye contact made Raj feel slightly uncomfortable and he bowed down his head and pinned his eyes to the ground.

"You…yes you!" she said addressing Raj, 'Stand up!" Everyone's eyes moved towards Raj. "Tell us about your hobby?" she looked intently at Raj, waiting for his response.

Taking a deep breath, Raj stood up from his chair and paused for a second. "I don't have any specific hobby, mam, but yes I do love playing sports." Raj replied after a little deliberation.

"Now, what I want to tell you is that it's good to pick up hobbies," she went on dramatically, "but" after a pause, she spoke again in a sarcastic tone, "I want you to forget everything for the next 4 years. Forget the world and focus on your studies. Focus on where you want to see yourself four years from now." All students swallowed hard.

Raj was neither excited nor worried at the Professor's words. He constantly kept thinking about the fun that he was going to have, the friends he was going to make and the cherished memories that he was going to create for the rest of his life. Little did he worry about the marks or the hard work that the professor referred to.

*

Life has an interesting way of teaching you that chasing success is no way to achieve it – for that to happen you need to figure your own interests rather than trying to emulate someone else.

That's what Raj did!

He didn't have any impressive academic credentials to get into a prestigious engineering college. Under those circumstances, his admission in Mechanical Engineering to the University of his choice was almost improbable. Yet he did get it in Regional Engineering College, Surat.

Raj went ahead to do what he loved to do the most, and followed it with all his heart, while at the same time he had a sense of optimism about the future. It was as simple as that.

He refused to be hung by a thread when it came to studies. He did not want to dig himself into an academic hole that was difficult for him to climb out of. Neither the desire to be successful nor knowing how anyone else did made the slightest difference to him.

Some of his co-students demonstrated their academic competency. Raj didn't fit that bill. He never had. He enjoyed hanging out with friends, doing things randomly, and nobody stopped him from wasting time or pressurized him to study.

*

Happiness burst into Raj's mind on seeing the dark clouds gathered in the sky. Cool winds gushed into the classroom, banging the windows. Sitting on the extreme left of class near the window, Raj leaned back on his seat looking outside, a bored expression drawn on his face.

"Raj!" An authoritative voice suddenly boomed out.

Raj was jolted out of his reverie. He had been so engrossed in his thoughts that he had forgotten that he was sitting in class, hadn't noticed the tall figure walking up to his desk. Very little of what Professor said, had registered in Raj's consciousness. His eyes skittered to the destination of that voice.

"Are you making a note of what I just said? Have you written down the (Thermal) equation."

He blinked at the Professor, confused.

Comprehension slowly dawned. "Oh, yes…yes Sir…. I am making notes." Raj said mildly.

Professor shook his head, as if he'd never heard of such an absurd thing before.

He looked across the desk at the pile of books resting on the table, his gaze hard and sharp. "Really! You haven't even opened your book yet!" "You will fail in your exam; this is a very important equation."

Raj looked at his desk. Even the books looked at him as if they did not want him to disturb them from their resting position.

"Ah…" Raj was at a loss of words." Sir, I was about to…." He fumbled as he tried to dodge the question.

Thankfully, the campus bell rung, signalling the end of the class. Raj heaved a sigh of relief.

"What the hell were you thinking?" His friend asked who was sitting next to him.

"I was thinking why do I need to remember the equation, is it to get marks?" The friend looked at him in amazement.

The professor dismissed the class, and the doorway filled with departing students. Raj moved towards his friend sitting behind him and exclaimed under his breath, "Look at the weather outside! It's about to rain. Let's go to the canteen and have Bun Maska- & Chai."

"Yes." Replied his friend with a spark of happiness in his eyes. He smiled and whispered the same to his buddy sitting beside him.

The three boys exited the classroom, chatting as they strolled towards the canteen.

"Wow! I love this weather! Look at the sky! It looks so beautiful!" Raj said with a smile plastered on his lips.

As they entered the canteen, they were greeted with other boys.

"Hello guys! How are you all?"

"We are all good. Wanna join us for tea?"

"Yeah sure! You all seem to be bunking the lecture," Raj said mischievously.

"You bet!" he bubbled enthusiastically.

"What are your plans in college and subsequent life?" a friend asked.

Looking through the vapours of the Chai as he took a sip of it, Raj shrugged, "Nope, I have no interest in planning at all." He scratched his head in contemplation. "Maybe…. maybe I……I haven't given it a thought yet."

His friends, mouth fell open. Goosebumps rose across his arm. "Hell…. what…what are you saying? You've got to be kidding me!"

Raj silently stared at him for a moment. After a moment, he burst into laughter. His laugh was deep. Unlike many students of the class, he had no specific plans for life. Over time, this feeling had settled in well, and he was satisfied with things the way they were.

"Don't laugh," his friend said abruptly, with eyes narrowing. "I am serious, Raj."

"Okay," Raj finally said zipping his lips and gaining control on his giggle.

Another questioned quickly, "C'mon, you must have thought something at least?"

Raj's expression changed. His happy smile faded to a frown. Raj cut him short. "Listen!" He paused; I rarely do anything with planning." Raj said with a note of annoyance in his voice.

"I see." He didn't look amused. "Dude, I really find it a little hard to digest that someone can even go on with life without an aim. Please don't get me wrong……" He exhaled a long breath.

"It's okay." Raj replied calmly. He chose not to banter back and forth with him. "It's not worth my time." He told himself.

"Bro, Raj is like this only. Totally chilled-out!" so saying he gave a double high five to Raj with both hands and the boys howled with laughter.

*

In college, everyone knew Raj as the guy who never cracked a book but managed to pull required grades. He was carefree, loved to laugh. His friends called him "Mahan". He got this tag as his views of life or philosophies were considered Idealistic. He always said "Life is simple we complicate it with our own Mind" "Life is all about Enjoying."

Quite early in college, Raj realised that there were several students who were smarter than him in various ways. Surprisingly, that never felt unreasonable to him. Even though he was surrounded by high achievers, he never felt the necessity of being exceptional or reach their levels.

*

As final year and final semester approached rapidly, the whole campus got on a different mission, campus placement.

As the campus placement season kicked off during the final year, the discussion around jobs seemed to occupy most of every engineering student time. The campus was abuzz with a list of companies visiting that year. Students rehearsed how to sit, speak and gesture during the interviews.

Raj's mind also dwelled on the forthcoming interview.

*

Raj sat on the couch waiting for his turn.

The tension in the room was palpable. Everywhere he turned, he saw worried students revising notes, mentally reviewing their profile and some of the accomplishments which they wanted to convey to the interview board. He shook his head in a rather bewildered manner.

"How ironical," he thought.

"First we have to rush to get good academic grades and then run a race to get a fancy job package." Raj thought to himself.

"Am I also going to be one amongst them?" He contemplated gloomily.

"No," said an inner voice. "This is not for you."

Still the big question remained the same: what would he do after graduation?

"I will probably think about this later." Raj told himself.

Raj waited impatiently for his turn to come, which it did in about ten minutes, although it appeared an hour to him.

After the greeting and a simple exchange of pleasantries, the interviewer questioned, "Mr. Raj, the first question I ask is, "What is your ultimate career aim?"

Raj gave his best honest answer. "Sir, there is no ultimate aim. I don't plan much. I live a life full of doing things that I enjoy." A dark eyebrow lifted in amazement. His face was impassive. There was no mistaking that the panel was not impressed by his candid answer.

As the interview was over, Raj felt like he was walking out of prison. He understood that he was not going to get selected.

*

The first three years of college had passed with lots of fun on the side. Bunking classes, eating out, watching movies and night outs were the order of the day for Raj and his batch mates. However, now the realities of life stared at them in the eye.

Given that he hailed from a small town in Uttar Pradesh where there was terminal shortage of high-paying jobs, Raj knew that a lucrative job-offer would be a great launching pad for his career. Of course, money too mattered. A pay cheque would help him financially. He valued money. He knew the worth of hard-earned money.

But the bitter truth was that he didn't want his life to revolve around a single goal of earning as much money as he could. His basic requirements were very minimal, and he was confident that he had the capability to earn the amount for the rest of his life and maintain his lifestyle.

At times, looking at his friends he wondered if there was

something wrong with him. Was he a misfit? Why was he so content? Was it good for him? And what were his goals? Was he too young then to understand life's goal?

He got no answers.

5. Entering the Door of Corporate

Sail Started in Ocean

A new chapter in Raj's life started on 26th August 1991, when he kick-started his career as a trainee engineer at Great Gas Co. (GGC).

It was here where his textbook life ended. This was the part where he entered the real world.

*

Raj boarded the train from Bombay Railway junction to go to Ankleshwar, where Great Gas Company, was headquartered.

He took the window seat and turned his attention to his co-passengers. He struggled to keep his sleepy eyes open, as he glanced through the crowd of people on the platform. Since the days of his childhood and youth, he liked to sit on the railway bench, and watch all the people rush about, run here and there to catch their trains.

He used to wonder about the mad rush of people running to

catch trains. He even weaved stories about them as he watched them come and go. His mind used to then wonder about them, thinking that they all had a destiny to reach to and he didn't.

Suddenly, the memory was replaced by a sense of realization that he now had to go on with his quest after all, that this was surely the time to begin.

As the train left the station, he closed his eyes, and within a few seconds his mind wandered, drifting and swirling like the wind. He surrendered himself to his thoughts that replayed the events of the last few hours.

He had dropped Ketan to the Mumbai airport earlier that evening. Ketan was going to US to study MS.

Saying goodbye was hard.

Ketan and Raj had been best friends. They had been together from elementary school all the way up. Raj felt a rush of nostalgia for his best friend. He had good reason to look back on their friendship with fondness, perhaps even with love.

Ketan had always been a true and trusted friend. He had always been there for Raj without an ounce of pretension. Raj recalled his past days. He remembered all the trouble they got into, all the times they laughed so hard their stomachs hurt. The times he had been there to listen. There was a lot to remember. And now he was parting with his best friend. A feeling of strangeness and solitude came over him, as he bid him a bittersweet farewell.

He stood stone-faced as Ketan waved goodbye at the airport, heading out into a new world. Ketan had wanted study in US ever since he could think.

Raj heard a voice and felt a tap on his shoulder. He opened his eyes. It was the ticket collector.

'Ticket Please?' The Ticket checker demanded, standing in front of him.

"Oh! yes, I have one." Raj replied, as he started looking for the ticket in between his wallet. The TC checked the name printed on the ticket, handed it back and moved ahead.

With an exaggerated yawn, Raj stretched his arms out over his head. He dragged his mind away from Ketan and his thoughts caught up with the scenic beauty passing by his window. He watched each and every tree that he was leaving behind.

He was happy at the thought that he got a job. What he did not know then was that he had joined India's largest, Private city gas distribution company, and that he would be spending ten years of his career with the organization.

*

He moved quickly to get down from the train, rubbing his head a little to collect his thoughts. It was already 9.45 p.m. He looked around for a few minutes before finding the way to the exit and then suddenly came the strong gust, rain-heralding. At this hour of night, he could not think of any suitable alternative for his stay in this rainy night. So, he decided to spend the night in retiring room at Ankleshwar Junction railway station.

The following morning, he got up very early. The excitement of starting a new job prevented him from sleeping.

A plethora of thought raced his mind as soon as he opened his eyes to the morning, and he looked forward to his new journey. The sky was cloudy, but not so cloudy that the sun didn't have a chance.

He looked outside the window and smiled, reminiscing

about the time in college when his friends used to say, No motivation! No passion! No dreams! He felt proud at the thought that he'd managed to wrangle a job before the University results were declared.

He had no clue about the new corporate world and its ways. The thought made his stomach churn. Till then, he just had a slight idea of how scientists worked, as his father was working with ISRO. As a child he'd seen his father working hard, committed to his job and sincere. Regardless of the challenges which seemed to be apparent, he was eager to contribute to his family income.

Dressed in his favourite blue shirt and black trousers, Raj set out for the first day of work, prepared for the challenges before him. He hurriedly headed to take an auto rickshaw. It had started to rain. Luckily, he had an umbrella along with him.

Raj had always loved rain. Unlike most other people, the sound of falling raindrops was one of the most acute sources of optimism for him. The sound of the thunderous black clouds in the sky made him believe that something beautiful was about to happen. The lightening which struck up the black sky convinced him that it was a glimmer of hope

It was not a long drive, barely three kilometres with morning rush-hour traffic, but to Raj it seemed hours, till he at last found himself standing outside the unfamiliar gate of his office.

Once again, he felt a surge of anxiousness twist his stomach.

As he made his way inside the building, Raj took a quick look around. It was the first day at work; naturally Raj was a little jittery. He wasn't sure what to expect. He felt that kind of nervous feeling in the pit of his stomach when you start something new. He looked in awe at the gas pipeline network in the midst of the office campus.

A lady in admin department, named Preeta introduced him to various department heads as well as the General Manager. The General Manager greeted Raj and took the time to review a brief orientation plan which the company had prepared for him. He was indeed impressed by the detail of the plan.

He spent the second half of the day filling out paperwork/joining documentation. Later, he was asked to familiarize himself with the agreement clauses between the organisation and the customer.

Raj had never been part of a professional team before. This was his first chance to be a part of a team that was open to everyone. He found that the people who worked there knew their job, and everyone was always on top of their work. Raj remembered how the whole family made Anar together as a team. Raj felt himself nodding as he smiled at the company's supportive culture. They were very nice and welcomed him with open arms. He found that they were open to any suggestions and ideas. That instantly made him feel comfortable and he thanked God for his blessings.

When the day ended, he felt peaceful and happy.

*

Over the next few days, Raj spent time understanding how the operations worked.

Things began to flow well, and he started getting the structure of the new position. Going into the position, he understood that he would be working with different end-users to ascertain their level of satisfaction with the organisation.

He was assigned the task of meeting customers to seek feedback on any issues they faced with the services of the company and ensuring receivables. Though this profile was not in line with his specialisation, he saw it as a challenge to stretch his potential and broaden his horizons.

For the first few days, he started accompanying a senior manager to various clients. A dedicated auto rickshaw and a driver had been assigned for visiting customers who had their factories in Industrial zone.

Raj found this idea very innovative as the rickshaw drivers were very well-versed with the routes.

During client interactions, he noted and learnt conversational strategies with new acquaintances and established customer. The exposure and the learning he gained were immense. He learnt about the most important skill the art of communicating.

As children, we learn a set of rules for proper participation in conversation. We learn not to speak to strangers who engage them in small talk. Conversational strategies of the corporate world are a different ball game. To begin a conversation with a customer, you must start off small; that is, start with small talk, to build that initial trust and rapport and then move to talking on agenda of the meeting. Small talk could involve any non-controversial topic: news, weather, events, politics, health, movies etc.

He thought that it was a wonderful approach! Guided by his supportive managers, Raj mastered this skill of communication along the way and was able to put his customers at ease. He quickly built meaningful professional relationships and adapted to the various situations he faced

Leading up to the final days of his internship, his responsibilities grew significantly, and he got used to the high-pressure environment. Tight deadlines encouraged him to become more agile and effective at work, which improved his analytical skills. He started enjoying meeting customers, solving their issues.

Supportive managers invested in his growth and kept pushing him to learn and apply as much as he could in order to deliver his best.

During that period, all he wanted was to go with the flow of life, and experience what it has in store for him.

6. Introspection

Sailor Lost in Ocean

Raj's days became monotonous. He sat at his desk staring at the bunch of invoices that needed to be cleared with the customers.

Three months had passed, and things- had begun to get real. The monotony of the job was beginning to get the best of Raj.

Raj's thoughts wandered, he started to think about matters that kept invading into his mind: what he was doing here? Why was he here at all? Was it supposed to be this way?

He'd been at this job for a few months, and he began to think about those aspects of the job that he enjoyed and found stimulating, and the ones that totally numbed him with boredom. He began to think about why some tasks bored him, and whether the interesting bits of the job were outweighed by the boring bits. He began to wonder if he should consider a career change - perhaps another work would engage him more and keep him from being bored like this. Or maybe he should gain some new skills - perhaps this profile was not aligned to his interest and that was why it was tiring him.

Raj took a deep breath and sat back in his chair, a smug look on his face. He had been on the field all afternoon and was now exhausted. Lost in thought, Raj didn't notice a colleague standing in the doorway of his cubicle.

He reached for the paper weight lying on the desk, he started spinning it. He watched into its depths as if his entire focus was on the small bubble of air trapped inside the glass ball. When the paperweight stopped spinning, he looked up and found the eyes of his colleague fixed on him intently.

"You okay, Raj?" The expression on his face was a map of worried lines.

"No. I …. umm. Well, yes. I am fine. I think…." Raj said earnestly.

"What's the matter?" he asked. "You look disturbed." His voice and his face grew kind as he spoke.

"Tell me…" he said unhesitatingly. The colleague's' face softened into such an expression of sweetness, that as hard as Raj tried, he could not hold in his emotion.

"Oh, I'm not sure," Raj sighed as he tried to organise his thoughts. "It's just that…. I feel…dulled with monotony of work."

The colleague listened attentively and then said with a sudden stealthy softness into his voice, "Give it some time. Don't worry."

Raj wanted to believe that.

Minutes later, Raj rose to his feet heading in the direction of the canteen for a cup of coffee. As he neared the table where his friend sat waiting for him, he almost tripped over himself. He gave a cry of anguish, almost going headlong but recovering his balance at the last second.

"What's wrong? Where are you lost these days?" His friend shrugged.

"I'm bored, that's it." Raj laughed merrily as he seated himself in one of the chairs. "The designation of Trainee Marketing is bringing my spirit down."

"What is it about the designation?" his friend queried.

"You don't understand," Raj drummed the table with his fingers. "When customers see the designation on our visiting card as Trainee – Marketing, they treat us as a fresher and do not respond appropriately to us."

"Yes. Yes." his friend sighed. "But that cannot be changed, right?" he pointed out gently.

Raj knew that something had to change, but he didn't know where to begin.

*

It was another beautiful monsoon morning, finer than the one before. He laid awake, staring at the ceiling. He had not slept well the previous night, knowing the day would bring him the same disengagement from work. He could not afford to doze off since he had many customer appointments lined up for the day.

"Was this why I studied for a degree in engineering?" He wondered aloud, his voice breaking through the calm silence of the morning. The only answer was from the thundering cloud outside, which at that very moment roared defiantly.

He made himself a cup of tea, and started to pace, struggling to keep himself alert. Taking a sip, he walked over to the window and enjoyed the drizzling rain.

He decided to scan the local news to take his mind elsewhere. He read whatever news his eyes fell on. But that didn't calm him much. The thoughts were getting to him.

He hadn't shared the stress or the anxiousness with anyone in his family. Why would he add to their worries? Dad was already stressed out enough. And Mom's on-going health challenges made sharing the troubling situation unwise, or at least unwelcome. But today, he wanted to set aside his nerves and uncertainty and open his heart to whatever he had within him. He decided to talk to his father and telephoned him.

His father's reaction was "Don't be a fool, you have such a good job in hand. Keep trying, and eventually you will succeed." Raj wanted to believe that.

"I am trying!" said Raj. "But the thing is…. it's so repetitive!"

"So what?" His father said in an accusatory tone. "Stick around and compromise; just like I have done all my life." Father said flatly.

"OK." Raj swallowed the lump in his throat.

The conversation ended up as: "I – I guess you're right Dad."

7. Aha Moment

Learning to Adjust the Sail

We all have had those "aha!" moments in our lives, time when a sudden revelation surprised us with an insight that changed our attitude towards everything.

For Raj, this moment happened with a seemingly insignificant meeting with his first mentor.

*

The intercom rang. It was the HR Head, Mr. Ram.

"Hi Raj," said a male voice on the other end of the phone. "Meet me in my office at 05:00 pm today."

"Yes Sir, Ok," Raj responded quickly. "I was actually looking forward to –" The call had been disconnected.

Raj looked at the phone trying hard to figure out the reason. "Why would he want to meet me at such a short notice?" he thought to himself.

"Why are you so happy, Raj?" A colleague asked, as he passed by the cabin.

"Ram called. He wants to meet me!" Raj mouthed happily.

He had heard a lot about the HR Head and had always wanted to meet him. Ram had a good reputation. Everyone in the office was impressed by his vision and actions, ability to organise people and move them forward.

"If HR wants to see you, then it may not be good? Hope all is well?" the colleague narrowed his eyes at Raj.

Raj got a bit of sinking feeling in his stomach. "You're right. Why would he want to meet a trainee who had joined the organisation recently?" he responded meekly.

A train of thoughts drifted past his mind. "Did I do something wrong?" Raj thought aloud as he massaged his temples.

He pondered to the negative possibilities of the meeting. He replayed the message of phone again and again in his mind, to interpret the meaning behind the words said by Mr. Ram.

He looked at his watch. It was 4:30 pm. He still had thirty minutes to go. Glancing at his watch again, he walked to the canteen to grab a cup of coffee. He took a long sip, enjoying the sensation of the hot liquid passing downward from his throat.

Minutes later, he walked slowly in the corridor, his palms sweaty, his face flushed. He nodded to his colleagues and made his way towards HR office.

The cabin door was slightly open. Raj's heart skipped a beat as he prepared himself for the conversation ahead.

"Hi, Raj," said Ram and extended his hand to Raj with a strong and firm handshake.

Raj's face immediately lit up and he felt comfortable.

"Hello Sir" Raj said.

"It's good to see you," you can call me Ram, he, began with

a smile that was bright and genuine.

Raj found himself trying to seem confident, as he passed a weak smile.

Ram, now comfortably seated in his seat, looked across the table and continued, "How are you?" he asked with a smile and friendly look.

"I'm okay. Work has been keeping me busy. I guess that's a good thing…." Raj trailed off, not knowing exactly what to say next.

"It is," he replied. "It helps you move through." He didn't need him to explain that.

"Raj, I'm sure you're wondering why you have been called to the office."

"Yes. I am." Raj said softly.

"So, Raj,' he said, "It has come to my attention that that you have concerns about your job title of a trainee. Wasting no time, you'll be delighted to know I'm going to change your job title. Your designation is no longer Marketing Trainee. From this day forward, I am changing your visiting card to Marketing – Officer. So, how does that sound to you?"

Raj's guarded expression changed. "Oh, that's wonderful!" he exclaimed, with a tone of incredible gratitude.

"You don't know how happy that makes me. Thanks." he replied, as politely as possible. The HR manager waved his arm in the air and flashed a smile of acknowledgment to Raj.

Just then the phone on the manager's desk rang. He excused himself, "Give me a second, please." He spoke to someone on the phone in a slow, deliberate voice.

Raj, in the meanwhile, could not refrain from wondering,

"How did the manager know? Had a colleague told him?" He had never once given any indication to anyone.

His thoughts were interrupted by the manager's voice. "So, let's get it started...huh...let's talk about your job. Tell me, how's it going?" He asked, looking at him knowingly.

After an uncomfortable silence, Raj chose his words carefully and replied, "As usual." He wondered if he had sounded as pathetic as he felt.

The manager gave him a bit of a questioning look. "As usual?"

Raj hesitated a reply, "Yeah, as usual." He let his words hang in the air.

"Are you happy at your job?" His gaze searched Raj.

Raj pulled himself up as straight as he could and threw his shoulders back, trying to look more confident than he felt. "I'm happy at my job, but maybe not fulfilled…." Raj recounted thoughtfully.

"The manager leaned back. "Tell me about it."

Raj straightened and shrugged. His thoughts were in a tangle. He wondered if he should be honest with him.

And then, Raj said, "I'll be honest with you. I have started finding my job is monotonous, there is nothing new." He paused at that point. The manager said nothing, but Raj saw his head nod as he waited for him to go on. "I don't find any meaning in my daily work. It's very repetitive. There is a lack of meaningful contribution to the organisation! It feels so unfulfilling." He lamented.

For almost a minute, Raj wondered if he had said too much.

Pushing his chair back, Ram looked at Raj, shaking his head

slowly back and forth and staring right into Raj's eyes.

The manager folded his arms and frowned, "Look, as to the monotony and repetition of the work, it is indeed easy to find a remedy for that. Move beyond just doing."

Raj gave the manager a doubtful look.

"What do you mean?" Raj's face assumed a puzzled, questioning expression. "Move beyond just doing…."

"That's correct," he confirmed. "What I'm trying to get at is this: you are an engineering graduate."

Raj listened intently, trying to grasp all that he was saying. "Have you ever thought of extending your knowledge base beyond your marketing role to understand the technical aspects of the gas industry, what are the different processes, and how the entire backend operates?"

Raj considered the question, and then shook his head in a motion of dismissal.

To me, what you need to do is simple: you must combine the customer problems with your technical expertise. This gives our customers the benefit of your knowledge and experience about the issues or problems.

A couple of minutes passed before Raj's mind gradually awoke to the approach.

This was true, Raj realised suddenly. I should combine information from different sources within the context of my own tasks. I should have a proactive understanding of the way things works! This was learning, not just narrowing the work to the role given but using education and knowledge to broaden horizons of work.

*

The manager broke the silence that followed. "Now let's move on to your second concern."

He added, "Your mention of a 'lack of contribution' made me think of something that might explain what I'm getting at. Let me put it this way."

He looked at Raj, "You've heard the story—we all have—of the five blind men and the elephant?"

"The anecdote that you and I have heard, goes like this. Five blind men were walking along the road when they came across an elephant. They had never seen an elephant before, neither had the concept of an elephant been ever communicated to them."

Raj nodded in acknowledgement of what the manager had said.

"So, they gathered around this animal and each of them grabbed a different part of the beast. Then they argued about what they'd seen. One blind man felt the elephant's ear and said he'd found a large leaf from a palm tree—the kind of large, flat leaf used as a fan. The second blind man had the tail and said he'd found a rope. The third had the elephant's trunk and said he'd found a hose. The fourth ran his hands over one of the elephant's legs and said he'd found a large tree trunk. And the fifth blind man touched the stomach and he said he has found a wall."

"And what do you think the story teaches us?" Ram asked.

A few minutes passed.

Suddenly, everything clicked and made sense; everything 'fitted'. An entirely new perspective unfolded before Raj's eyes. That his organisation was a complete elephant, and he was contributing only to the part of it, whereas if he sees the whole elephant he can contribute more. Now he could see the complete view, full picture, 360 deg. vision whereas he had seen before only part of it.

"This was it. This was the missing link – A HOLISTIC APPROACH!" A holistic approach is what every professional should have, where not only mastering your part of elephant. We should learn how it completes the whole elephant, how big a part it is of the whole elephant and how important a part it is of the whole elephant. The elephant must be visualised in each stage of work, the role, the design, and the organisation as a whole.

Immediately after exiting the office, he headed for the washroom and splashed several handfuls of cold water onto his face. He stood looking in the mirror. His eyes lit up. He smiled at his own reflection and waved a hello to the new person he was.

*

Raj was happy and the perspective made him even happier. And as he walked back home, the evening breeze found him whistling happily to himself.

He realised that the HR manager had given him a new vision on how to view his daily interactions as being part of an interconnected whole.

"Yes, he's right!" he thought with a smirk.

"I can see it now!" He nodded to himself. No one can see the complete elephant, but each one chooses to "see" only a part of it, each from a different angle of view – incomplete perceptions of a more complex reality. The opinion of each one may be true, but it is limited because of insufficient holistic knowledge.

"The big thing," he told himself, "Is to have the knowledge of whole elephant instead of part of it. Ram is right. I could not grasp the complete elephant. I only could comprehend part of the whole."

*

Little did Raj know that the meeting with the HR manager would give him clarity of vision that would penetrate every decision in his life. Little did he know then that the HR manager's name would be etched among the caring people who enriched his professional life forever.

Little did he realise at the time that this new approach of holistic thinking would resonate with his temperament, his profession and it would open a new chapter in his life.

8. Living the Holistic Approach

Setting the Sail – New Destination

Life gives us many situations in which we lose our comfort zones long before the new opportunities are revealed to us.

It's scary!

*

Raj quickly started mastering the new holistic approach, seeking to understand the business from inside-out.

The benefit of this approach for him was that senior managers in sales, operations, quality, and engineering took an interest in mentoring him. They willingly answered his questions; thus, he got to learn the business from many perspectives.

Raj applied that learning to his day-to-day work. He was becoming well-prepared to facilitate discussions among customers and soon got opportunities.

This approach became a big hit with existing customers. Before this, the field officers were focussed on fielding questions on service-related issues and then giving them to someone else to follow up. This holistic approach decreased customer complaints- a problem that had fostered for years.

It happens sometimes. You get an opportunity, and you find yourself caught between your old ways and new.

You are torn between the two paths. You know that whichever path you choose, you'll be nurtured by it. But you also know that the experiences you'll have on either path are very different from each other.

So how do you decide?

Raj did not know it then, when a new job opening presented itself in Ahmedabad in the newly formed New Business Development (NBD) department of the company.

Thereafter started a new battle within Raj to continue in the existing job or step out of his comfort bubble at the current office and expand his skill set.

It was a battle between the easy choice and the right choice.

He recalled the words of his grandfather and in silence he repeated them. "When given a choice, we always opt for the simple option. Naturally, this is what we want to accomplish. We constantly yearn for life to be simpler. Pleasantly simple. Easy is soothing and simple. But occasionally the simpler option ends up being the incorrect one. Making the simple decision could seem like the option that will make us happier, but it may not provide the exposure needed in the workplace. On the other side, if we choose wisely, we may strive to live better lives. The choice between the two is a difficult one. They are at constant fight with each other. They resemble the angel and the devil who talk to you while sitting on your shoulders. Each one wants you to listen to them. One would always choose easy over right if asked to make a choice."

He then understood the wisdom of what his grandfather had once told him.

*

Raj paced the floor whole night-deciding, and then changing it.

A little later he then went back to the window and looked outside. Between him and the world was the glass and behind the glass – the green fields and the road. He looked blankly out of his window to the street below. It was the road he knew. He knew it all by heart, every twist and bump on the road.

The two thoughts played tug-of-war with him but brought no solace of satisfaction to help answer his dilemma. He didn't know if he will be running away from something, or if he was heading to a specific destination, for a particular reason.

The analysis of the new opportunity showed the interconnectedness of various elements that formed the larger system for decision making. It gave clarity on the professional front, about the new department, its purpose and contribution to the organisation, its leadership and management, its team, his potential role and responsibilities.

He took a deep breath and made one last attempt to refocus on the situation at hand.

He closed his eyes once again and saw the vision of his mother and his father-he would get to stay close to his parents if he took the new offer. What it would be like to be back at home? He missed his parents, especially his mother, and the benefits of being close to his parents in Ahmedabad couldn't be measured with anything else. He was satisfied that it would give him opportunities to think about marriage.

Thinking holistically, he finally made up his mind to apply for the job opening in the New Business Development of the organisation.

And he was ready to take up the challenge.

*

Raj's mind was made, holding on to more parts of elephant, he would take a lateral shift in the New Business Development department of the organisation.

He decided to take a few weeks to better familiarise himself with the roles and responsibilities of the new position. He needed to determine whether the apparent challenges he had identified were real. He researched as much as he could about the department and new role. His research gave a fair idea that the new role matched his expectations and allowed him to prepare himself for the application process.

He met people from the department to figure out what the day-to-day workings of the position would entail. Since the movement was within the organisation, he got the opportunity to advance his knowledge and skills with much lesser effort as compared to an external job change.

So, he took the plunge, willing to be uprooted from his comfort zone and planted into a new culture to do a job for which he had little training and experience but gave a holistic approach to his vision.

Raj did not know then that this would be one of the most consequential, life-changing decisions he ever made.

9. Life at Its Best

Sailing Far wind with
strong Helm

There's a saying, "Find a job you love, and you'll never work a day in your life." Raj was blessed to find that job when he got transferred to New Business Development (NBD) at Ahmedabad. Not only was it recognised as a great place to work, but he was also an integral part of a department that was recognised as one of the "Best Places to Work" in the organisation.

*

Raj woke up with a start wondering whether he was dreaming of the melodious saccharine voice of his mother or was her voice for real. Was it a dream or reality? The sound of his mother reciting prayers fell in his ears. The fragrance of incense touched Raj's nostrils.

Was he really in Ahmedabad!

He looked around his bedroom in a daze and murmured half aloud, "Home, sweet home!"

He snapped open his eyes and sat straight up in bed. He

yawned and looked through the window at the sun shining brightly in front of him. "Wow! It looks like it must be a beautiful day."

The delicious warmth of the sun rays playing upon the floor of his room made his inner spirit active to start the new chapter of his life with bliss.

Today's the day, he thought. Let's do this.

*

Raj had been appointed as the senior engineer, of New Business Development (NBD) of Great Gas Company (GGC).

When you're new and inexperienced, you want to work for someone who is willing to encourage you or inspire you down the road. Someone who is willing to explain things, who has a precise vision with clear expectations. Someone you can see serving as a role model or a mentor.

Philosopher and self-help author Bob Proctor describes a mentor as 'someone who sees more talent and ability within you than you see within yourself, and helps bring it out of you.'

Raj found that person as soon as he started the new role.

His interactions with Mr. Krishna (He was fondly known as Krish) made him realise that the man was a transformational leader who relentlessly inspired, convinced and guided team members to achieve the desired outcomes. He was a strategic thinker who would look at the bigger picture. He was always very transparent and accessible. He was rational, approachable and would openly speak up with everyone. He was an empathetic leader.

The man, who later became Raj's mentor.

Raj realised that indeed, a strong leadership affects the entire organisation in a powerful way.

*

Soon, the company shifted focus from natural gas to LPG (Liquefied petroleum gas) business. LPG industry was liberalised by Government of India, which motivated private sector to enter.

Raj was part of the team of business development. This was the golden period of his job.

He was a part of the strategic business planning team. There were two major activities involved in this; one was the creation of the strategic business plan for the next few years, and the other was the implementation of that plan.

Working on strategic planning gave Raj immense learning opportunities. It opened his eyes to the various webs of relationships within which the organisation exists. It also opened Raj's eyes to the competitive advantage that the organisation had. Fascinatingly, strategic planning process enlarged his vision to a holistic analysis and development of a larger organisational picture in terms of project implementation, operations, distribution channel, target markets and return on investments.

Blending theory with practical application, Raj underwent in-plant training to understand business operations.

Two bottling plants project came up, one in Rajkot and the other in Ahmedabad.

Raj was the project engineer at Rajkot plant, and he was assigned the responsibility for two units in the bottling plant. Soon the project winded up to its completion date. The two years of focus, dedication, and willingness to spend the time and energy to develop the new project paid off for Raj. His team went on to become the most successful team within all business units in key performance indicators. They surpassed their targets on most measures, becoming a star team.

The project conclusion was marked by a huge inauguration ceremony that was organised for handing over the completed project to the operations team.

*

Raj and his mentor, Krishna were travelling from Rajkot to Ahmedabad by car.

Watching the other cars pass by their face held the hint of a smile. It was a happy moment for Raj and his boss. They had successfully accomplished the task of bringing the project to the finish line.

"I expected good, but the outcome of this project was great." Krish said aloud in an enthusiastic tone.

"Raj, you there?"

"Hmmm…" mumbled Raj.

He had been so engrossed in his thoughts; He was happily thinking about last few months on this project work. He was remembering his first mentor who had given him concept of holistic approach (vide) elephant parable. He was contemplating how this approach would have made execution of this project more effective; he didn't have the faintest idea what Krish had said. "Oh, I'm sorry, uh, Sir, what did you say?"

"The team did a great job; don't you think so?" he spoke to Raj.

Raj "Yeah.uh, yes, of course!" "There were so many milestones to celebrate throughout the pilot, and we have all learned a lot along the way."

"What do you think was missing in the project?" asked the boss.

The question came up so suddenly that it caught Raj momentarily off-guard.

He took a moment to collect his thoughts. "I think that what was missing in the overall commissioning of the project," Raj said slowly, carefully choosing each word, "was that we were doing too many things at the same time; there were too many people involved, and the type of work we were doing was in different directions. The team could not see the entire picture of the project, that's why they were disintegrated."

"Continue." requested the boss, stroking his chin in deep thought.

"The problem I thought— is that we all worked on the project like blind men. We destroyed our possibility for coherence in the project, because none of us had the complete picture of this elephant." Said Raj

"As a matter of fact—" continued Raj, "each team member was looking at just his part of the project. One managed the pipeline implementation, the other managed the storage tank implantation, while the third managed solely the hydrant, and someone else managed the bottling section. Each one was only looking only at their part of the mystery. But nobody looked at the elephant in its totality!"

"That sums up rather nicely. So, you're telling me that we are in the same situation as the various blind men, and we saw no better than they did?" The boss shot him a glance. His voice held a teasing note. "Oh! This means that I have all blind men on my business team who can't see the elephant!" The boss laughed and laughed as though he hadn't heard that story before. "The elephants are the key to our future aren't they!" He laughed even harder at this one.

"No!" Raj said, smiling cheekily. "I... that was not what I meant." he said red with embarrassment. "All I was saying is that they need to be reminded to pull all the pieces together." Raj ran his fingers through his hair pushing back his hair as he moved in his seat uncomfortably.

"I'm sorry I couldn't resist! You should see your face!" He was grinning and when their eyes met again, he let out the sharp laugh that he was holding back "Come on," he said, his voice chiding. "I was just kidding."

The boss let out a whiff of air from his mouth and said, "That was one of the best laughs I've had in a long time."

He shook his head grinning, "You're right young man. We did not apply your elephant principle in the project," said the boss, "and that was the missing link?"

Raj looked both relieved and disturbed at the same time, but he laughed a little along with the boss anyway.

"Absolutely! That's right!" said Raj mirroring his reaction.

For a moment, there was silence between them.

"Yes, well—okay, you're right, Raj," said the boss after a pause. "We'll work on that one…"

The car suddenly came to a screeching halt, followed by multiple car horn honks. "Damn! We're badly stuck in traffic." Raj adjusted his posture against the car seat, and he looked out the car window

"Relax, Raj." The boss grinned broadly as he faced Raj.

"Tell me Raj, what do you think you could have done differently to make everyone see your elephant?" he asked.

It took him a few seconds for Raj to answer the question,

but when he did, it was from a practical standpoint.

"I just feel that like we could have been better if the elephant had been defined. Each department could have focused on the Elephant rather than individual department" And...." He paused for a moment and looked over at his boss to see his reaction.

"Yes," said the boss, before resuming the conversation on the bottlenecks faced in the last project.

"Also, our vendors should be better handled with better co-ordination of activities." Raj added.

"What about our third-party safety certifications? Would you say we did right, or we did wrong?" questioned the boss.

"Wrong," Raj said after a moment's thought.

For a moment Raj was silent. "Well, the point is, in the safety inspection by the third parties, what was crucial was getting certifications on time. We wasted lot of time in the audits."

Raj looked at his boss to see his reaction thus far. The boss smiled at him.

"So, how do you propose a relatively smoother transition in the next project?"

Raj enthusiastically outlined the various suggestions for project improvement. The mentor listened intently. He then massaged his left hand over his mouth and chin and looked away, as if silently contemplating some important question.

"In view of these facts from the previous project, it seems to me that a holistic view of the project should be adopted." Raj said in a confident tone.

"Raj, after listening to this extremely well-thought-out plan, seeing the detail with which you have analysed the project plan and put together the future action plan, I am even more impressed."

He again congratulated Raj on his hard work, his overall plan, and his enthusiasm.

"Thank you, Sir" he said with a gleam of pride in his eyes. "I appreciate your support." He felt a lightness and joy in his heart. He had finally done it!

"We're in this together." He supported Raj, "Let's do whatever it takes to make sure that the next project is every bit as successful as we've planned it to be."

Raj smiled happily at the feeling that his ideas and his efforts were validated, and that he was personally valued and supported by his boss.

The journey from Rajkot to Ahmedabad had been exhausting. Raj reached home late. An intense feeling of weariness fell upon him. Once he reached his room, he collapsed onto the soft bed without even removing his clothes and closed his eyes.

This time there were no dreams.

Only deep sleep.

*

He woke up early the next morning, feeling happy and hopeful for the future. He went over to the window, seeing the bands of light on the white curtains. The sun had risen. He stretched himself in the rays of the warm morning sun.

He smiled as he took a deep breath as his mind immediately started to replay the events of the previous day. A pride peeked out through Raj's eyes as he thought to himself, "I'm so lucky and thank God for graciously sending him in my life as my mentor."

He fondly thought of his first mentor, Ram, in Ankleshwar, who started him on the journey to holistic thinking and to help him develop the necessary skills to adopt it.

He smiled as he replayed the words of appreciation of his second mentor, Krishna, who gave him the opportunity to apply and reinforce holistic thinking in a business context.

He recognised the significance of this milestone. "This," he told himself, "Is really success!"

But Raj's success didn't stop there.

10. Sweet Taste of Success

Sweet Sailing

They say one success leads to another success.

After completing the Rajkot project, Raj felt that he had achieved something big. But life had not yet erected a monument; it had simply laid the foundation, broad and deep and secure, as a pedestal on which the finished statue of his career was to stand.

*

"She seems to be a homely girl." Said Raj's mother giving her own approval, while all other members of the family nodded in her favour.

"She's good looking also." added his sister with enthusiasm. "Her photograph has impressed me." "Don't tell me you haven't noticed, Raj?"

"Yes," he replied.

Raj was sitting comfortably looking outside the car window. He was travelling from Ahmedabad to Vadodara with four of family members to meet a prospective girl for marriage.

Raj was in an introspective mood. Everything had happened so fast. Everything had changed. When he had left college, he was a carefree collegian. Now, marital responsibility was staring him squarely in the face.

At every other milestone he encountered before, the next step was always clear. Now it was anything but clear. Change was coming and Raj was powerless to stop it. If it cannot be stopped, it must be embraced, he thought.

His thoughts were broken by his brother-in-law's voice. "The girl is a doctor!" There was a tint of pride and achievement in his voice as he spoke.

"What difference does that make?" Raj uttered with his usual cool and determined tone. "What most important is that she has to be professionally qualified and non-career oriented."

"I'm happy to know," Raj's father said, "that you've very clear thinking about your life partner."

He was right.

Raj had clear notions of what his partner will be like. He did not know how she would look. One thing he knew for sure: the woman with whom he could live under one roof must be intellectually beautiful. He didn't want a woman who was married to her job.

*

Raj, surrounded by his family members was sitting in front of the girl called Radha. Around her were members from both the families busy in talking to one another.

Raj threw a glance at the girl. The first thing that he saw of her, out of the corner of his eyes, was her long hair, big eyes and bony cheeks. Something else too struck him. She looked quite simple. There was a glow on her face, a very warm and pleasing glow.

Impressive, he thought.

Raj got an opportunity to interact with Radha. Neither of them knew how to start the conversation. Radha sat speechless; her eyes fixed immovably upon her toes.

Raj broke the silence first. "If you have to leave your job and stay in a small city with me, what will you do?"

She was utterly amazed by the question. "I don't know," she said honestly. "I've never actually thought about having to quit my job."

"Could you?" Raj persisted.

Radha thought about it for a minute. She looked at him keenly as if to judge his true meaning. "I will happily go with you to the city and use my degree to do social service." She said, flashing a most dazzling smile that lit up her face.

"Great!" Raj said, as a smile crept onto his lips.

They exchanged a few more lines when the time of interaction came to an end.

After the formal conversation and refreshments, Raj's family was ready to take leave of them. Raj heard his sister speaking to one of the host ladies that they would convey their decision to them very shortly. She thanked Radha's parents for their hospitality and spoke to Radha for a while before leaving the place.

The host family walked up to the main gate to see them off. Raj felt all the eyes were focused on him. He gave a smile with folded hands till he got into the taxi. He was at peace and felt optimistic as the taxi wheeled away.

On the way back home, there was a smile on the faces of

each member of the family. Signs of hope were written all over their faces, they started discussing about Radha. The whole family approved her in all respects.

Raj too gave his consent.

He was very satisfied, even though the decision was taken so quickly. His intuition and feelings had made the decision for him. He felt that that the choice that his parents had made for him was perfect. It was as if God had chosen this woman for him. He desired to spend the rest of his life with her and make their relationship official.

The next week was spent in fevered preparation, for a hasty engagement the same week.

The engagement was a brief, yet elegant affair with family, friends and office colleagues. The guests were left awestruck by the austere decoration. It wonderfully reflected the romantic ambience of the event. Raj took special care of every detail as his mentor, Mr. Krishna was among the special people who were to be present for the occasion.

There was a look of pure joy on Raj's and Radha's faces during their ceremony. Radha looked like a dream at her engagement ceremony. The glow on her face and her smile said it all.

The wedding was scheduled after seven months.

The more Raj came to know of Radha, the more he saw of her beautiful soul. He realised that she had a very quick mind that could help work out the problems of life.

He realised that she was the sweetest, most intelligent woman he had ever known. Her personality was everything a man could hope for. She was strong when she needed to be and submissive when appropriate.

He couldn't be happier. All he thought about was how sweet the journey of life was going to be from then on.

It already was.

*

Raj was overjoyed. He was given the responsibility of leading the bottling plant project of Ahmedabad.

On hearing the news from his CEO Krishna, his mind was in ecstasy. Raj was full of confidence, vigour and ready to start immediately and joyously.

When Raj came home that evening, he broke the news to his wife and mother, they both stared at him with their mouths hanging open in happiness. Radha's heart swelled with pride as she wished him congratulations. He was anticipating words of praise from his dad. They never came and the silence hurt. He longed to see a gleam of pride in his dad's eyes. It would confirm that he truly was successful.

Raj lay on his bed looking at the ceiling in a contemplative mood, as if he were deeply troubled by something.

His mother walked in with a cup of hot tea. "What happened?" she asked seeing the dejected expression on his face.

"Mom, why can't I ever please dad?" Raj asked.

The intemperate childishness of his words made her smile a little. She assured him that his father was equally proud of his success, as he was with all the previous milestones.

Raj looked at his mother with a puzzled look. "Previous ones! When was I successful earlier Mom?" His mind grasped for an explanation.

"You always were a successful kid." she said, with a gentle

reproach.

Raj gave her a slow searching glance. "In what way?"

The first success came when you were thirteen-year-old and got admission in the eighth grade in a school like St. Xaviers. When you made those anars of perfect dimensions, that was success! When you got good grades in tenth grade and got admission where you wanted, that was a success. You were a successful youngster when you got admission in the engineering college of your choice without paying a single rupee of donation." She paused for a moment, as if to fact-check herself.

Raj's eyes were fixed sternly and questioningly on her face. "You mean—" he began, then paused. Then, in a changed tone, he went on: "Yes, you are right, Mom."

Mother continued "When you got a job even before your college results, that was success."

He stared intently at his mother and nodded his head in agreement.

"It's your little success story!" she said with a warm smile.

"Success does not mean income, you know. Nor does it mean the position you have reached in life. And in no way does it means getting ahead of everybody else." She spoke softly, calmly, yet with conviction.

All these little milestones along the way—was success, my dear! The last words were spoken intensely, with deep feeling. Raj smiled at his mother as she squeezed his arm, her eyes warm and glowing.

What a feeling—he felt successful!

11. Visulaise "The Elephant"

Sailor is the Artist where Wind is the Medium

It doesn't matter what industry you are in or how proficient your employees are, people will and can innovate if they are able to see the bigger picture and are able to comprehend how they contribute to positive change. Clarity about purpose and goal go hand in hand.

This is what Raj did – showed his team the connections, how they fit in the bigger picture.

*

The meeting in the conference room hadn't started yet, and the six people around the table were all glued to their laptops. They had officially been a team for around two years in the Rajkot project and had indulged in brain storming sessions on several occasions. But in the new project, the team had been restructured by their leader Raj, and their responsibilities well-defined.

External experts for mechanical engineering were done away in favour of an internal team-member with years of expertise in pipes, pumps, compressors, and pressure vessels.

The project team was waiting for their leader Raj to turn up. He had summoned them here for a team meeting.

There was a sudden burst of energy as the door flew open. Heads turned towards Raj, their new leader, as he raced into the room and greeted all with a smile.

"OK, let's get started. We have a lot to get through and not much time." There was no chit-chat going on, which meant Raj could get started straight away on his list of agenda topics.

Going around the room, each of the team member was asked to give an individual update. This was mostly in the form of a dialogue with Raj, and no one else intervened. He continued to move the agenda along, listening to each person's update, asking some questions, and then moved on to the main agenda of the meeting.

He walked towards the centre of the room. "We've been working together as a team for almost two years now." He looked around as all the team members gave him a brief optimistic smile. This new Ahmedabad project is important to the company, right, everyone?" All heads nodded. "So, are we all ready to make this new plant a success?" Everyone grinned and gave the thumbs up sign of success.

He paused. Everyone waited expectantly to hear the rest of what he had to say. He cleared his throat and continued. "We all agree that there's was a wealth of industry experience in this room?" He looked appreciatively around the room. "And" Raj continued, "each and every member here is unavoidably an expert in his own domain." Raj looked around the cabin at each of the team members. Without hesitation, all were nodding in agreement with the positive assessment.

Raj shook his head firmly. "But…" he paused again. Everyone waited for his continuance. "But what Raj?" What could he possibly say, everyone wondered.

He added in a lower voice. "Sometimes even a successfully completed task could be the starting point for an improved method of doing a particular job." The smiles dissolved into furrowed brow. The team members all stared at one another and then turned to Raj,

"We're going to use the background of the Rajkot plant to understand an important concept that we probably missed out then and apply it as a lesson in the present project."

There was a confused murmur among the people present. "Missed out? What on earth are you talking about!" challenged a team member.

'Yes, we were all wilfully blind to one important thing. We saw only what we needed to see, and thus we were all blind…" Everyone shook their heads and shrugged, to show that they did not understand.

"I don't understand a thing you are saying, Sir," a team member said.

"Neither did I until some time ago," Raj said looking straight into his eyes, "until my first mentor told me this mantra of success, that I am going to share with you today." His expressions were sparkling his eyes. He looked into the distance, looking back in time and reviving a precious memory."

He cleared his throat and addressed his team, "Let me simplify it for you."

We all know the story of the blind men and the elephant in which each described the part that he could touch. The blind person who touched the elephant's leg said, "The elephant is like a column." The person who touched the elephant's side said, "The elephant is like a big wall." And the man who touched the ears said, "The elephant is like a fan."

"That's a funny example Raj." said a team member as he looked thoughtfully at Raj.

Raj smiled. "Because the blind person cannot see the entire elephant, any conclusion and judgment he makes by touching only one part of the elephant will be limited. A blind person had only a small part of the full picture. But what if eyes were given to see the entire elephant?" Each blind man would stand amazed that the whole truth was larger than his original vision.

"We see the project in the same way the blind person "sees" the elephant." He paused and looked at every one of his team one by one with unusual intensity.

Some frowned; one or two bit their lips; others looked confused and searched Raj's face for any clues. His bright, brown eyes had softened, but their misty depth seemed impenetrable. "Don't get me wrong. A few minutes back, each one of you gave me an update that was on a part of the whole. But can anyone in the room describe the whole project?"

Silence.

"I think I understand what you're saying about the importance of a bigger picture," said a team member.

"We need to see the whole picture, don't we?" said another team member sitting at the far end of the room.

Raj paused for a second and then said, "Yes, we need to conceptualize operations of our project on a broader stage. We must broaden our outlook by collaborating with each other. When we collaborate, we can see the whole elephant." There was once a firm and decisive look in his eyes as he spoke, without any hesitation or negligence. There was a determination.

He glanced at the team and spoke in a very serious tone of

voice: "I now wish to put a question to the collective wisdom of the meeting; you are looking after pipe designing at the site, you are looking after storage tank, you are looking after pumps, you are looking after hydrant…. aren't all these just functions that contribute to the overall make-up and success of the project. Shouldn't we look at the overall project instead of having a myopic view of our work?"

The people sitting around the table seemed to understand by the last statement.

When he spoke again his words were "Each blind man came away confident that he knew what an elephant was like. We're like these blind men. We can walk away thinking we have the right amount of knowledge; our knowledge could be limiting the reality."

The team exchanged incredible and happy glances.

A team member gave him a questioning look and asked, "Is this concept of elephant really relevant?" "Do you really believe that this story from granny's bag of stories can be applied to! There was a slightly sceptical note in his voice. Raj didn't take offense.

"You doubt it?" Raj asked him in return.

"Quite a bit, actually," the team member replied in a carefully neutral tone.

"I appreciate you telling me this, and I won't blame you for thinking that this concept is irrelevant in the professional world. But, my colleagues, I must tell you that it is just as relevant today as it was years ago and should be required reading for professional success." Everyone listened with rapt attention.

"Let me tell you something very personal…..." Raj said in a low voice, as he leaned across the table. Everybody, now fully attentive, anxiously waited to hear what the new leader had to say. Raj waited a few moments before he shared the story with the group. "Some days back, he smiled, "I was one of you. Today I stand before you, in charge of commissioning this project......only and only because of vision of elephant!"

He nodded decisively. "That's how relevant this elephant is in today's world."

He got up from his chair and walked carefully towards the whiteboard and filled it with some dots. He stared at the whiteboard for a few moments, and he put some more little, tiny dots randomly on the whiteboard.

"Each of us sitting in this room," he said, "is representing part of Project. Just like each part of elephant represents your respective department, the whole project is the Elephant."

Then, he drew a line to connect dots together. As he connected the dots first the legs then stomach, then tail, then ear, then trunk and finally the whole elephant emerged.

It was suddenly clear.

There was a picture!

Wow! The team gasped in disbelief and awe. They were blown away by what had become of all those dots. They understood to see the elephant rather than only its parts like their own departments. For a complete project success only their department achievement was not enough. It was to be hand in hand for all, to bring success of Projects, ensuring seamless organisation

It was like someone had made them hear an entire song. Each instrument in the song they were listening to have a specific role to play, and each voice was a necessary component of the whole.

They smiled, eyes shining with admiration.

Raj's eyes began to glow beneath the soft overhead light in the conference room. He looked around at the faces of his fellow team members and seemed satisfied THEY HAD GRASPED THE SIMPLE CONCEPT OF HOLISTIC THINKING.

"Okay, team," Raj said. "Let's get started. Good luck everybody."

*

Ten months forward, the second LPG plant was successfully completed and inaugurated by the CEO's wife. Both the bottling plants at Rajkot and Sanand near Ahmedabad of the company were commissioned in the previous year and maintained an uninterrupted gas supply to its customers.

Raj was happy and his efforts were appreciated. His wife Radha looked at her husband with pride as she held their toddler daughter in her arms during the inauguration ceremony of the second bottling plant. She had been a big support to him managing the house, her job, and the new tiny member of family, while Raj gave all his energy and time for the Projects commitments.

He had progressed professionally, and his career had started doing well, very well. He became the area manager. He had success written all over him. He took up challenging work assignments like handling operations and sales by appointing franchisees of various cities. Raj rose to positions of greater responsibility.

He slowly and steadily grew in his knowledge, experience and contributed whole heartedly to the organisation. As a star performer, his imprint was all over the company. Respected, admired, and envied. He had brought growth to the company and was admired for his innovative thinking.

From a purely technical person, Raj could become a techno-commercial person, just like his second mentor.

His heart would swell with pride each time his mentor would tell people, "This guy knows how to carry the organization very well outside the organization!" He humbly acknowledged to himself, "I have reached this position probably because I had best mentors at the centre of it all."

There was no stress in work now. Together, he and his wife had set up a beautiful home. He looked joyously ahead to a happy life with his wife and daughter—the apple of his eye.

What he didn't know then, was that life would change in the blink of an eye, casting a long dark shadow—a shadow that would stretch over several years.......

12. Lost Vison in dark clouds

Sail hitting the storm

A feeling of insecurity of job ran high in the minds of most employees that they were going to be laid off and Raj too had been very apprehensive since he'd sensed that big changes were in store at work. He ran through various scenarios in his mind, contemplating his next course of action.

There had been an organizational change wherein the company was bought by a British company. This new company decided to sell out LPG business and expand operations into natural gas projects.

He finally decided it was an opportune time to move out into natural gas business. And he asked for a transfer to natural gas, and it was sanctioned almost immediately.

The move seemed the right fit, and the transition happened faster than he could have imagined. Raj moved to the head office of Great Gas in Ahmedabad and became a part of the new projects.

During that time the Company received authorisation for its new natural gas pipeline that started in Surat district and terminated in Bharuch district. Raj was made a part of this project and he was given the responsibility of project management of this pipeline. Hereafter the path of Raj's career altered forever. Everything that happened in his life after this was different.... completely different than he had ever anticipated.

Things would get better from here on–or so he thought–incorrectly.

*

Here, then, he found himself caught between the horns of an increasingly painful dilemma. On one Project, Raj was a highly competent project manager of a project; the next he was operating as a member of the group's pool of project staff.

On one Project, Raj was giving orders; the next he saw himself taking directives from a Project Head, which he was simply expected to implement. Raj thought that some of those directives were counterproductive. However, the Project Head was both high-handed and indifferent to any of Raj's increasingly inadequate attempts to influence him towards holistic approach. The person in question used an increasingly unsupportive style when dealing with him, denying him influence and reducing his views to trivial and irrelevant.

Raj struggled a lot to cope with this changing workplace dynamics, feeling of devaluation and the quest for influence area. Devastating his mental peace and irritation kept creeping in all the work areas. Raj often found himself wondering whether he had made a desperately reckless decision by moving to natural gas. Raj tried to console himself with the thought: what choice did I have, and I can still apply my holistic approach and contribute to organisation. Despite all my expertise in project operations, the company would not have let me manage operations of Natural gas. Privately Raj always knew he was trying to validate the decision he had made, a decision that, as he now learned, had destroyed everything.

One decision. Why hadn't he agreed to go Ankleshwar or Surat in Natural gas? Why had I allowed to refuse all the offers outside Ahmedabad? Why had I insisted to stay in Ahmedabad and not leave my comfort zone? He got no answers.

Standing out in the balcony of his room, staring out at the void beyond, all he could now think was you have lost the most important thing in the world, your self-identity.

Now there was just no escape. There was no solution.

Against this backdrop of negativity, dilemma and disappointment, Raj continued to work in the project-not as productively as before, but with the same level of originality and determination to go his own way. He was frustrated, more than he wished to admit. He felt vulnerable, as if everything had come to an end, as if now, here, at the very moment, he was nothing but a tiny man in a black suit, riding on a fragile bird. He felt insignificant and diminished.

The changes in Raj's behaviour and his perpetual gloominess were familiar to everyone who knew him well. People knew something was wrong with him, but there was a battle within him, that no one could see.

Day after day, he battled to continue with the normal tasks in a way that wouldn't expose his struggling inner self. His problems increased. What was a simple task for him earlier, seemed an uphill task in this journey of lifelessness, emptiness and being lost. He felt like an injured soldier, stumbling through a smoke-filled battlefield, trying to save himself from the enemy bombs, searching for some escape from all the madness.

His life was spiralling out of control.

He started facing difficulties initiating communication. Difficulties in reciprocating emotions. Difficulties in expressing his point of view. Difficulties in understanding others' perspectives. Difficulties in sharing ideas.

The man who was extremely knowledgeable in his own field and master in translating his thoughts into words, now had trouble articulating himself before people.

Raj was lost.

The damage was done.

*

"My point stands. I cannot do this!" said Raj to his colleague Suresh. Raj's face was impassive, but his jaw grew tighter as he spoke. His anger and disgust were evident as he looked at the points on which he was told to make a presentation. "None of this makes any goddamn sense!" Raj's voice boomed through the office.

Hearing the loud sound, the Project Head came hurriedly from his cabin, "What's going on? Why are you shouting Raj?"

Raj looked up sharply and snapped loudly, "Don't–you–dare–talk–to–me–in– that–tone– you–understand?"

The Project Head gave him a long hard look. Something wasn't right with Raj; the outer edges surrounding his brow had dropped more than he could remember, his expression now holding a perpetual emptiness and sadness.

He heard a hollowness in his voice, a lack of strength that was never there before.

"Okay. Relax. Come on tell me, what happened" he said softly, trying to pacify Raj.

"Suresh wants me to make a presentation from this," Raj said with sarcasm in his voice. "Read this," he said and held it out to the Project Head. "I'm not going to do it, that's final." His voice reached a high pitch as he spat out.

The Project Head took the paper looked at him, brows furrowed. "What's wrong in this?"

"You really think there is nothing wrong in what he's written?" Raj said glaring at him fiercely. "Wrong! Everything is wrong! That man doesn't know his job."

Raj was talking so fast that he couldn't grasp the details of what the problem actually was. All he could gather for certain was that Raj needed help.

It was easy to see that Raj wasn't going to listen to anyone, and whatever the Project Head's directives were, he didn't want to follow them.

The Project Head tightened his lips. "For God's sake Raj, lower your voice and stop getting so worked up-it's such a simple task that he has assigned you!"

"Wow really!" He snarled leaning forward until his face was inches away from the manager. He made no attempt to hide the resentment that he felt within.

"You know what…" His jaw was clenched. "I am going to give that man a piece of my mind. Until then, don't say a word. Not one word, okay?" An expression of impatience coloured his face as he waived his hand dismissively.

His mouth opened, closed, then he repeated the process twice more. He started to walk towards the Project Head's office when he abruptly stopped and looked back.

Then suddenly rose a storm of despair and conflicting emotions in his heart. He clutched the door tightly as if he was holding on to life. "I-I can't. I can't handle this." His voice quivered, as he banged his fist on the closed office door.

"Where's my phone?" he demanded aggressively, "I'm going - home," he said. "I won't be back." He walked unsteadily towards the exit door. It seemed as if he was about to collapse. He gripped the ball-shaped metal doorknob tightly, drew in a final deep breath and turned the knob.

The hard line of his shoulders eased. His eyes moistened, and after a protracted silence, he dropped his gaze on the floor, unable to look anyone in the eye. A small sound escaped his clenched lips, "I can't, I can't…."

He walked out of the office slamming the door behind him. "Don't follow me," he blurted out with an angry glare at the office staff watching him.

The day was complete now.

*

Minutes later, Raj drove back home. The drive was one of silent contemplation. His heart was broken, his soul fractured. The feelings of loneliness had resurfaced.

The traffic light turned red, and he grumbled to himself as he rolled his bike to a halt. He rubbed his temples with both hands. He inhaled deeply and let the breath seep from his lips while he tried to swallow the lump in his throat. He hadn't been able to get much sleep for days.

He felt as empty as the landscape in front of him. He turned his head to look at the corner of the street intersection, where trees and dead branches lay toppled across the ground due to the hailstorm. That seems just like me, he said to himself.

He was snapped out of his thoughts by the sounds of the

long line of vehicles honking impatiently behind him.

Honk! Honk! Honk!

It took him a split second to realize that the light had turned green.

He couldn't move, his gaze fixed straight ahead.

It was as if all strength went out of him. His head started to spin so intensely that his vision became blurred. His eyes filled with tears from the pain of the internal battle of what is right and can help progress and what was in his control to do it. His pounding heart said it all; the emptiness within him that was choking him, and the truth was, he needed help.

He shook his head wearily, as he ignored the cars behind him honk ceaselessly, then edge past as their drivers glared and cursed angrily. His face remained blank and expressionless.

After about five minutes, he put the bike in gear and drove full speed up towards his house.

He pushed open his bedroom door, slammed it shut and closed all the curtains-keeping the world, and all its inhabitants, locked out for eternity.

13. The Family Hold on

In MURKY rough waters

He felt like a cornered animal fighting for its life with all odds against it. There was simply no way to escape from all the people sticking sharp sticks in his cage. He wished he could turn his back on the entire situation and pretend the past few months at work hadn't happened.

He had in the past appeared to be on the brink of a nervous collapse, but this had all the makings of "the big one."

*

That fateful day was different from others.

Unlike every other day, Raj had returned home early. His head was heavy as if someone had kept a huge stone on top of his head. His mind was trapped in a box of images. As if everything came to an end. As he banged the door of the room shut, Radha rushed to the room.

"At least talk to me," Radha pleaded. Her voice was soft and compelling.

He leaned toward her, growing pale. "I'm not sure what to

do anymore." Raj rubbed his face wearily. His eyes became blurry, and they kept squinting all the time.

"What happened?" She urged. "Raj! Please answer my question." Raj couldn't find the answer, nor did he understand the question.

He looked thinner and paler; his splendid eyes, which were fixed on her, were sunken. He looked almost like he was fighting back tears.

He stared at her with a look almost of fear. "I have come back," he said with constrain, as he crossed the room and stood with his hand tightly clutching the back of a chair, as if trying to force his body back under the control of his will.

"I will not go back there." He scowled angrily and muttered something that Radha could not catch.

"Go back where? Raj! Please, for God's sake, tell me!" Radha pleaded. She looked at him, trying to catch his eye, but he wasn't making eye contact.

He seemed uncertain where to begin. "My mind feels -" He broke off, chewing on his lower lip, staring into the distance. A look of confusion invading his face.

The look in Raj's eyes made her sad. Those eyes had no love, no beauty, no dreams, no hope. They did not shine and the sadness, the heaviness, the bitterness seemed to be pouring out through his eyes.

"I don't know what has happened to my mind," he whispered, staring at his wife without a blinking.

Radha hugged him and pulled his head onto her shoulder. She couldn't remember a time when he was this vulnerable, and it took all her strength to push down the lump in her throat. "It's okay, Raj. You've been through a lot. You need to just give yourself some time."

He was silent for a minute, then he asked slowly as if he wasn't sure how to form the words.

"Where…. where is the washroom? Where is the washbasin?" he repeated. Radha was speechless with the question but led him to the wash basin. He washed his face and the moment he saw himself in the mirror, all the hidden tears reassembled in his eyes. There was no more running away from himself; the tears started to flow freely as they had when he was a little child. He sobbed inconsolably.

Radha was startled at his behaviour. She did not know what was happening. She flattened her hand on his chest.

She went to sit by his side, her arms around him, as he cried inconsolably. "You will be fine." She hugged him as tightly as she could, all too aware that they were both trying as hard as they could to somehow believe the words she was saying.

*

"Now, Raj," the psychiatrist said, "I want you to rest and relax for the next few days. You do look very tired."

"Yes," he said, as though it was the first time it had occurred to him about how tired he was. "I do need to relax." His dark brown eyes looked to a faraway place. His fingers tapped impatiently against his thighs.

"Maybe this is what I need." He almost whispered the words and began to clasp and unclasp his hands in a very agitated way.

Radha cast a glance at Raj watching the almost uncoordinated movements of his body, as he rocked back and forth in the chair. Then she cast an uncertain glance at her father-in-law, and another at the doctor.

Raj's father was trying to look as composed as possible, but his steady nerves had been shaken by watching his son's erratic mannerisms.

"I just need to know what's happening! Please, Doctor," he interjected. "We want to understand what is happening."

The doctor looked at the two of them earnestly. "Look," he said to Radha, "I need you to know that he is not quite himself. He is suffering from acute depression." Radha's eyes widened. Raj's father cast a frightened glance at him and seemed speechless with confusion. The doctor gave Raj one of his quick glances. "One thing to keep in mind," the doctor added, "He might broke down. He might hallucinate and see people you don't see. There is a possibility that he might come in and out of consciousness. That's perfectly normal, but it can be very disturbing if you aren't expecting it."

Raj's father gave Radha a distressed and apprehensive look.

Radha met the doctor's look, and she didn't know what he meant. "One thing to keep in mind," the doctor added, "he should be in solitary confinement for the next seven days. Come what may just make sure he eats his medicines on time." The doctor's eyes were warm and understanding. "I will see you next week," he said handing over the prescription.

Radha looked at the paper and nodded. Being a doctor herself, she knew where the doctor was going with this line of treatment. But deep inside shivering with unknown facts.

*

Radha couldn't sleep. She lay in bed with her daughter curled up next to her in the kids' room. Raj had gone to bed hours ago and her father-in-law slept in parents' room. Radha lay in the dark listening to her little one breathing and was scared & shivered how they would cope with this life alarming situation.

More than a week had passed since Raj's frightening ordeal. Raj had been a prisoner in his bedroom. His condition showed no signs of improvement.

She sighed heavily and reached over to tuck the duvet tightly around her little daughter.

A loud noise in the bedroom made her jump. She flung off her blanket and rushed to the master bedroom.

"You want to suffocate me in this cell, isn't it?" He stood up, unsteady on his feet, and he pointed at her. "But I will not let that happen." He hissed furiously going red in the face.

Radha's lips quivered like she was fighting with herself whether or not to speak.

"I hate you!" His eyes became fierce with rebellion.

"Damn it!" "I can't bear to stay here anymore!" He pushed the sides of his head with his palms and squeezed his eyes shut.

"Please...Please listen to me....", she whined.

"Raj..." "Raj," he said, mimicking her in a whiny girl's voice.

"Shut up! Just shut up....and stop playing these dirty games with me." He was clearly agitated.

Radha kept pleading. "Raj, I'm not playing any games with you," she told him.

She walked to the side table and removed his pills. "Come on, take this," she said with respect and love.

"Mind you, I am not eating any more of these. These don't work." His voice was flat. "Call that doctor right now and tell him. I'm stopping the pills. Period."

"No, you can't do that." A sadness crossed her face.

"And who is going to stop me?" His voice was harsh.

She looked at him pleadingly and said firmly, "Eat this."

"I will not, do you hear that." He crossed his arms and glared at her. Radha sighed. Her shoulders slumped. "Why are you being so difficult?" she said, as she laid her hand warmly on top of his.

For a moment, his expression changed. "You can't understand how nasty I feel each day after taking these pills. Every morning when I wake up, my body feels like an immovable weight. D-d-do you even know how much effort it takes, just t-t-t-to get out of my bed in the morning?" His voice was soft and pained. Dark circles rounded his eyes, and they were empty as they looked into hers. "Inside." He broke off. "I feel like I'm d-dy-dying." she heard a hollowness in his voice as he spoke, a lack of strength that was never there before. She went cold to her core.

"Oh, Raj...?" Reaching out, she gripped one of his hands. "We all love you. We'll get through this. Trust me, things will be better." It hurt her to hear him like this, but she was determined to see the broken glass as half full. She spoke summoning her full strength, exhausted and feeling defeated herself.

He shook his head. His jaw was clenched. Fear filled in his eyes. She could see it in his eyes - the layers of exhaustion, anguish, and pain.

"Give it time and you will feel better," she said, with more conviction than she felt. "Let me go and get you some apple juice to swallow your medicine."

As she reached the door, she turned back to Raj. "I think you're absolutely right. The pills are no good. I'll have to talk to the doctor about changing the prescription or dosage. And maybe, you may not need them anymore!" She knew that the last statement was a lie.

*

Holding back tears, Radha left the bedroom and closed the door behind her. She inhaled deeply and let the breath seep from her lips while she tried to swallow past the lump in her throat. She gathered strength in her legs and began to walk toward the kitchen.

She forced a slight smile and made her way back to the master bedroom with a glass of juice on a huge tray. Her head and heart were hurting so badly that she was hardly being able to balance the tray.

Raj gave her a sly, sideways look, and stared at her hand a bit as if he was considering something. Then he picked the glass of juice from the tray and balanced it neatly in his hand. "What have you added to this?" he sniffed and asked suspiciously. The edge in his voice was back.

"R-Raj... What are you saying?"

He threw back his head, with a deep laugh. "Didn't you just spiked it?" He stared at Radha; the tablets seemingly forgotten in his hand.

"Raj I-I... did not." she protested in shock, forcing herself to speak as calmly as she could, even though she couldn't stop her hands from shaking.

"Bet?" Raj smiled coldly as he leaned back against the head-board of his bed.

"For heaven's sake, believe me, Raj!" Radha whispered.

"I'm warning you. You lied to me yesterday too!" Raj's eyes

pinned her. "You think I don't know that you tried to drug me!" His voice trembled.

Radha shook her head in exasperation. "Please Raj," she said slowly, not knowing how to deal with it.

The room was possessed by a quietness.

Breaking the silence of the room, Raj said, "Show me it's safe," He sucked in a breath and pressed his lips into a tight line. "You drink this first," Raj stared out of the window, his jaw muscle clenching furiously. He was determined to not drink the juice.

This was the first time he had done this. And he continuously repeated refusing medications, food, and water; eyed it suspiciously; thought it was poisoned; dipped his fingers in the milk to check if it was drugged; believed that his laundry was being done separately - not with the family wash; and had a determined conviction that everyone was plotting against him.

But Radha wasn't the one to give up. She was with him, at his side, no matter what. She was determined that somehow, their love and medicine would bring the light back into his world.

She shook her head at him, misty-eyed, but determined. He placed the glass of juice beneath her nose, and he watched her intently with his dark eyes. She took it from him, sipping some of it.

When she glanced at Raj, he was eyeing her with distrust and unfriendliness. All colours had left his face. She leaned over to her husband. "No poison. None, never. Now have your medicine." She said faintly, realising that Raj understood nothing, not her words, not her feeling, not her tears, not her pain.

Raj's eyes moved back and forth wildly to an invisible object behind her. They finally rested on the family photograph on the wall. He remained silent for a moment, and the agitation in his heart now began to settle. He finally took the medicine with a sip of juice. The pill scratched his parched throat as it made its way down. He swallowed again and again, pushing it as far as he could until he couldn't feel it anymore.

Radha bit her lower lip and forced herself to hold back tears. The shape of his eyes had changed, and the outer edges surrounding his brow drooped more than she remembered. His expression now held a perpetual sadness, his mind muddled by sedatives and sleep and exhaustion.

It pained her to see him this way, and she prayed that the medication would take effect soon and he'd find his way back to the happy and optimistic man she'd married.

"I think you should leave," whispered Raj, interrupting her thoughts.

She straightened her shoulders and looked him straight in the eye. "I'm not leaving until you lay down and try to sleep."

"You didn't hear? Just leave." He said like a sulky schoolboy.

She took a calming breath and turned back.

Once she had left the room and closed the door behind her, Raj heard the soft grumble of voices from the hallway.

"Their conspiracy has started again," Raj muttered to himself.

How he wished the house were empty. There wasn't space for anyone or anything in the house, but himself and his thoughts.

*

"I'm not sure why," Radha started. "I really don't know why, but for some reason, Raj is convinced that we are all ganging up against him." Her father-in-law's- grip tightened.

"What do you mean, 'ganging up?'" She took a deep breath. "He's convinced that we are all his enemies." Saying the words aloud made her dizzy, and now she clutched her own hand for support.

"For God's sake, why would he think that?" He looked panicked, his eyes searching Radha's for an answer.

Radha touched her head with the backs of her fingers. "I know, Dad. I know. I tried explaining that to him." She paused and peered out the window. She wished things had been different. At least he wouldn't have been going through all this pain that he was at this moment.

"Is it getting worse?" he asked. "Are his symptoms getting worse?"

Her mouth stiffened. She didn't respond right away but then nodded her head slowly. She felt tears well up in her eyes. Life was hard and future uncertain with a small daughter, job and to take care of him with no clue of future. "He's going to be alright, isn't he?" He whispered. Concern etched his face and Radha could feel the helplessness of his father.

"Papa don't worry!" she said confidently, "He's got the best doctor in the city. It's just a matter of time."

"Time," he said softly, wondering how much more damage was being done to his son as they spoke.

14. Sunrays Gleaming though clouds

Hoisting the Sail

Several months had passed since Raj had resigned from his job. It was a roller coaster ride of unimaginable difficulties & hope, sadness and recovery, unhappiness, and unusual life. The depression had lifted-by a lot-but the residual symptoms persisted.

Raj would occasionally remain quiet and withdrawn. Sudden waves of anxiety and agitation would sweep over him, sometimes without any apparent cause. He would disappear on his bike and wouldn't show up for hours. His family would be scared all that time trying to figure out where he was. At other times, he would sit and stare at his food for several minutes. Worse still, stare at the tube light for several minutes and claim that he could break it with his energy by just staring at it. On some occasions, he would hallucinate about his deceased grandfather and father-in-law.

The man who had an amazing grasp of details, who never lost sight of the big picture, was engulfed in a sad state. His mental illness had made him lose sight of his vision, the bigger picture it represented.

*

Raj was tired. Tired of sitting on life's side lines, waiting for things to get better. He has recovered a lot now, the time elapsed and the gap that came in his professional career and growth did not make him sulk or feel frustrated. He believed in action; he was not a man accustomed to waiting. If only he could find a way to turn back the hands of time.

His emotions were all over the place: worry about his job, concern about the future of his wife and children. And, of course, there was the biggest fear of all, the one that made him shiver from the inside out: fear of the future. His thoughts seesawed at the realization that he was at a crossroads in his life.

He opened the window that looked into the dark street. He looked right, and left, and then right again. He looked again; a frown puzzling his brow. Suddenly, he wasn't sure which direction to look in. A nagging feeling came over him and he thought he should go in the direction suggested by his sister.

Raj's sister had advised that he should move out of the town, to another country, and start afresh. She suggested him to relocate to Nigeria where she lived.

He was still unsure of what would happen when he arrived in that country. But he knew that was probably the best option. He still wasn't sure if this was the best choice. A real sense of apprehension come over him. His head ached, and he could not force his mind to let go of its disturbing thoughts. Maybe he should move from Ahmedabad. Maybe he should move to Canada, USA or UK.

After a moment of thinking he nodded slowly. Although it was a tired nod, it was not a defeated one. It was the nod of acknowledgment coupled with the determination that he could achieve anything, anywhere in the world.

He lowered his head and nodded. Nigeria would be a better

option." He thought to himself, with a conviction growing in his mind. Yes, Nigeria was indeed one country where he can start again. He felt a particular affection and gratitude towards his sister.

The more Raj thought about it, the more sense it made. Only he was unhappy leaving their new-born second daughter, Mitu so soon.

"It's definitely, yes." Finally, he prepared himself for the day, for the coming hours, and for the future. Life must move on.

*

It was departure day. All around the room, Raj's belongings were packed into his suitcase.

His wife, holding a five-weeks old baby and an older seven-year daughter, stood next to him, looking at her husband in silence. He smiled at her winsome gaze, then dropped a loving gaze at the baby in Radha's arms. His face softened. "What a little darling," he said slowly, keeping his voice low and gentle as he looked adoringly at the baby girl.

He turned to his elder daughter, and reached for her, holding her in his arms. The baby went to him willingly enough, and soon gurgled with laughter, as he tickled her cheeks. And down his cheeks there rolled a big tear. He sobbed, as he strove to hide a tear. He looked at Radha and tried to read her expression, but he could barely see her face until she lifted her head and looked into his eyes. Her eyes were full of vulnerability.

Swallowing the lump in her throat, Radha wiped a few tears. "It'll be okay, dear," she promised and hugged him. He hugged her back, breathing in the fresh scent of her familiar perfume, already missing her.

He took off for the future before him, leaving behind the life he had known, and the lives he had brought into the world.

Looking down at the scattered city lights far down below, he wondered what Nigeria would be like.

He was ready to start afresh, and the dream of achieving professional success felt more closer than ever.

"Nigeria, here I come."

*

Raj started going through the vacancy ads in the newspaper, looking for a suitable job. This worked when he finally landed a job as Branch Manager at Divya Motors, franchisee of the Kia automobile in entire Nigeria. The company used to import cars from Korea, and they had the franchisee of the automobile in the country. Due to his rich experience in customer service, the company hired him to take care of showroom operations and deal with customers. He was posted in one of the company showrooms in Lagos, the commercial capital of Nigeria.

He took the job without hesitation. He was brimming with enthusiasm and optimism to be having success again in his life. It started to work, like a wonderful new adventure had begun. This was going to be his ticket to a new beginning.

He started getting accustomed to life in the new country. It was a challenge to start with since he did not have the relevant background in the sector. But Raj was a man determined to succeed

After some months in post at Lagos, Raj was transferred to show room in APAPA, Lagos to set up the new showroom. He took up his new assignment with determination and began to practice holistic thinking principles that he had learned.

He then moved to Abuja, capital of Nigeria and then to Port Harcourt, oil city of Nigeria.

He moved from city to city, meeting targets in each branch office that the company opened in Nigeria. However, just when each city has been reached and operations stabilised, the next city became his new waypoint, and he paddled off in another direction.

*

One day, he woke up in the morning feeling an overwhelming sense of homesickness.

Why did he feel so numb? What was this feeling as if something is missing from his life? What was happening to him?

He was on the threshold of everything that he had dream of when he started from India to Nigeria, yet he was unhappy. He could not put his finger onto the source. He was under no stress or pressure and his job was going well. Yet he sensed that something was amiss. His mind raced; there had to be some explanation, he was missing something very important.

"What could I possibly be missing?" Raj wondered aloud.

"I want to go home," he murmured, his voice sounded low and exhausted.

He pondered if his unhappiness was just a fleeting thing due to homesickness and loneliness, or whether there was a more fulfilling life in some other country like Canada or USA.

"It will work, it has to work," he said in a mumbled voice to himself, his teeth gritting tight in determination.

He reached office and walked inside the showroom slowly. There was something in his slow gait that told of impatience, and an anxiety to find something. He looked around, and the showroom was filled with people.

Thinking about home naturally led his thoughts to the family. Radha and his little girls were always in his thoughts, and all he could do was hope that God was listening to his prayers and watching over them for him. He wanted – he needed – to have access and closeness to his family, his children and their lives.

From a distance, the words "Come, come" called out to him. He gave a deep sigh. He wondered if Radha was missing him as much as he missed her while taking care of her daughter and parents and herself alone there.

He blinked hard. His chest tightened at the thought of his wife.

*

Raj sat in his office, staring into space. Restlessly his fingers rotated the pen over and over between his fingers. He looked up at the time. There were still few hours before he got off work. He stretched himself, gently sighing.

Over the next few weeks, his dissatisfaction grew almost to an obsession. After months of moving to different cities in Nigeria with a persistent die-hard attitude; and months of efforts to gain victory in the professional world, Raj felt disillusioned. The hope that he had nurtured to be professionally successful in Nigeria seemed to be falling away from him. He was tired of the stillness that had started sinking now. He wanted a new and fresh fragrance that would fill the gaps with its essence.

He started reassessing his job, his life, wondering if he had made a wrong decision. The more he thought about the matter, the more dissatisfied he became. And he seemed to be unable to quit thinking about it.

Raj decided it was time to talk to his wife. He ran through all the reasons why he thought Nigeria was not a good fit. She listened intently while he discussed the pros and cons of leaving Nigeria forever versus staying on.

Listening to his muddled thoughts, she finally said, "Raj, I don't have any doubt in my mind that what you are saying is right." He heaved a sigh of relief. Radha was always his biggest supporter with whatever he was trying to accomplish.

His mind had decided, and his heart had agreed to take the plunge. This was it. Now it was time for action. It was time to find a new life and a new map with a new destination.

15. Persevering on

Family that Sails together stays together

"The coffee is perfect, thanks," said Raj, setting his cup down. Raj's brother-in-law too set his cup and settled back into the chair.

Raj's brother-in-law lived in Kampala, Uganda and worked in a multinational cement company. He had suggested that Raj should relocate to Uganda. Adhering to his proposal, Raj flew from Nigeria to Uganda and started his new job. Radha was happy that she and kids would be joining soon with Raj.

Raj had been offered the position of Unit Head in an aluminium manufacturing unit named Aluminium Product Manufacturing unit (APM). The company was headquartered in Mombasa, and the manufacturing unit was in Kampala. Raj was sceptical about joining the organisation as it was not his domain. Besides it was a medium scale unit.

He now looked forward to the future with fresh hope and new zeal and having family next to him.

*

He was eager and excited about the new beginnings. A new

chapter. New life. He couldn't wait to start.

Monday morning arrived and he was more than ready.

Raj walked through the door at 8:45 a.m., arriving fifteen minutes early. "No way am I going to be late today," he thought to himself. "This time I'm entering this impressive office as the newest member of the manufacturing unit." He wore a brand-new navy-blue suit, red-and-blue striped tie, and a white buttoned-down collared shirt.

"Well, good morning, Mr. Raj." He was greeted by his boss's secretary. "It's so nice to see you here today."

Raj acknowledged "Good morning to you too. I'm really happy to be here."

"Please come with me, Mr. Raj. Mr. Sagar will be in shortly and I know he will want to see you first thing," said the lady as she directed him to a guest office to wait.

Mr. Sagar arrived and everything began to happen all at once. First, several key staff members were asked to join in the morning meeting.

Raj observed how disciplined the team and its leader were and thought to himself, "They understand what it means to value time."

As the brainstorming session began, Mr. Sagar took off his jacket and rolled up his sleeves, clearly ready to begin. "Now let's go over the morning agenda," he said. "By lunch we will have our business plan objectives defined. So, let's get started." "This is an amazing experience. I'm really happy to be part of this highly functioning team of professionals," thought Raj. "I still feel as if this is a dream."

As the brainstorming and the morning meeting evolved, he heard every aspect of the project challenges.

Within a period of three months, he familiarized himself with all aspects of operations.

*

Raj was trying to rebuild his life. He was doing it. It was slow, and hard, but he knew that he could and would do it. He shifted his focus to all the tangible things that needed his attention: learning about various aspects of the new job, meeting new people, learning new things. His colleagues and boss supported him as an individual and they made a good team. At work, he was respected for his knowledge and skills.

Life was a breath of fresh air, a dream compared to the past few years. In the simplicity of it was complete peace. His wife and children joined him in Uganda. No one was more excited than Radha. She was so proud of her husband, so ready to support him to be himself again. She wanted to start this new chapter of their lives together.

Raj soon reached a lifestyle that was ideal for many. A beautiful well-furnished house, an independent chauffeur driven car, and servants at disposal. He enrolled the children in one of the best schools, so that they could make the best of their life. Radha took up a job as a Medical Officer in a Trust Hospital. The maid would pick the kids up from school, bring them home and feed them. In the evenings, the family would go for tennis or swimming at a club. They would often have lunch or drink coffee in various clubs, coffee houses and restaurants. On most weekends, they would go shopping at the mall. On holidays they would go for trips and vacations. He couldn't afford most of the things the family wanted, but he could afford the things they needed. It was not luxurious living, but it was a good living.

Raj couldn't have asked for more.

He often looked back and remembered how life had given him a hard blow, but also how God had turned it into a blessing with his family who loved him so much and stood by his side.

The family really started to believe that they could be 'at home' in Uganda. The place had so much to offer families and individuals who enjoyed the outdoors. The city had many amazing landscapes, beautiful parks, historic monuments, endless forests with a variety of national parks which offered unforgettable wildlife experiences.

The weekend was here. Raj arose from a restful sleep with renewed energy. Radha made breakfast for the kids, who were busy packing their bags. The family had planned to visit to a wildlife sanctuary along with their friend Sam during a long weekend. The kids were very excited about the trip. They couldn't wait for the adventure to begin. The hours before the trip seemed to drag on forever.

During the safari, the kids saw all the animals they had hoped to see. They were particularly delighted to see chimpanzees and gorillas, lions, zebras and deer.

At one point, they had to suddenly pull their car to a halt. about 15 yards away, stood a herd of Elephants! They were right in front of the car and close. Everyone sat rooted to their seats for a moment. The kid's mouth remained wide-open. They had never been so close to something so huge, so wild, so fascinating! Sam quickly shushed them, and they pretty much held their breath as the herd walked by to the other side of the road, giving a good long look as they passed.

The weekend went by fast, and before he knew it, he was on the way to work again. Uganda was beautiful.

Mr. Sagar moved to Tanzania to set up a new unit there, and Raj was given the expanded responsibility of handling the entire operations in Kampala – from sourcing of raw materials, and manufacturing, to quality control, and sales of products manufactured. HOLISTIC THINKING INCORPORATED in the unit.

It felt as if everything was back to normal. Life slowly returned to normal ... but not for long.

*

Raj's positive outlook motivated his family to believe in him, and the fact that they would get their lives back on track.

But then one night over dinner, his positivity waned again.

"Papa!" his younger daughter ran up to him. He picked her up into his arms brushing her brown curls aside from her face.

"Hi baby," Raj gave her a kiss on the cheeks. "How are you?" he asked. Her brown eyes twinkled at him. He looked at Radha and then back at his daughter.

I am good she laughed.

"Good," he kissed her again. "How about we get some ice cream? We can eat it in the car while we drive around?" His daughter clapped her hands in delight and looked at her father with the biggest, widest grin. He called out to his elder daughter.

"Hey that's a great idea" A smile lit up his whole face.

They stopped at a faded yellow ice-cream van. He watched lovingly as his younger daughter smacked the ice cream with rainbow sprinkles. He gazed at his elder daughter as her tiny teeth nibbled at the chocolate and her tongue licked the vanilla that appeared underneath. The little girls smiled up at their dad as their taste buds celebrated the wonderful taste of the ice creams. Radha took her own lick of her single-scoop ice-cream cone. He stared at his family for a long time. His expression turned distant. He felt an ache watching them. He could have given anything for their happiness.

As he looked at them, his mind grappled with the thought of the higher education of his girls.

"Papa come and take a bite," his little one said excitedly. "Oh! Yes," he answered, as he walked up to her side and sat next to her. Radha smiled, she loved the way that her daughters were so close to Raj. He kissed their younger one on the forehead and then kissed their elder daughter as he headed back towards the car.

On the way, Radha noticed that Raj looked tired and annoyed, and she knew he was displeased with something.

"If only I could see what comes next," wished Raj. He seemed lost in deep, profound thought. A little wrinkle appeared between his eyes. A thought was beginning to take shape in his tired, fuddled mind. It was coming to him. He finished eating the last of his ice cream as he looked at the time.

Radha said, "Should we go home? We are already quite late."

"Well, maybe you're right" he muttered, and they started to walk towards the car. After a moment of what seemed unbearable silence, he said, "Yes, let's go home."

"Yes, let's get back home. We are already quite late." He repeated the words even more thoughtfully.

Satisfaction appeared in his eyes, but his face was still slightly taut.

*

The microwave dinged. Radha withdrew the cups and handed over one to Raj.

"What's wrong with you, Raj!" She asked, as she took a tentative sip of coffee. "I want my daughters to have best of the education" he said. "Our daughters can also take admission in any foreign University, once they are out of school." Radha said.

Something in his expression told her that he disagreed. With an abrupt shake of his head, he started to object. "No, not my daughters. Period." Raj said with disgust.

"Listen to me-this will be the last time I'm telling you this." He said in a firm tone.

She glanced at him. "What's going on in your mind, Raj?" He didn't say anything. His only reaction was to press his lips together. She could feel his anxiety, though his face remained expressionless and still.

"Give me time, and I will tell you." He eyed her steadily, considering.

"Unbending attitude," she said. "Well old habits die hard, I guess." he said. stopping the discussion on topic.

She looked at him and with softness in her voice, she replied, "I understand your concern about our daughters" She was starting to worry about the children as well.

He paused for a few minutes in deep contemplation. "Well..." he began, and then stopped without completing the sentence. He took a deep breath and then slowly said, "If we both think our children have nothing here, why or what are we waiting for?" Raj suddenly blurted out. "This place is not right place for us to live on for the future of our girls.," he retorted, frustrated to have to say it aloud.

Radha looked at him with surprise, trying to comprehend the meaning of his words. She realised how disturbed he sounded. "Can you tell me what happened, Raj?" She raised a sceptical brow. Her look was piercing.

His expression turned stony. "There aren't any Universities around, sadly." he reasoned. His throat tightened until it burned at the thought.

"You could say that" she agreed, as the overwhelming feeling of concern for her husband's health swept through her body. Raj has not been quite himself lately. She suspected he was a bit concerned, but more so, perplexed by the dilemma in which he found himself. Her heart flipped and tremors went through scared that his mind had started playing games or he really was analysing the future of kids.

"The educational challenges that girls face here are many. I have an odd kind of-of-." Raj paused with his coffee mug halfway to his lips.

Radha gave him a tentative smile, with fear and apprehension of future but he didn't smile back. There was concern in his expression. He looked worried as he began to think more and more about the destiny of his girls; that their educational pursuits would take them thousands of miles from home.

For a moment his mind drifted back to all the comforts of his current job, but he knew that the "material comforts were only temporary". It felt like there could never going to be any happiness in life without his darling daughters.

He decided that the best place to start over was where his kids would be safe, and where he could give them a good education. That place would be his home country, India.

"I'm ready," Radha murmured and smiled sadly though she wanted to discuss the decision he was taking. Her gaze roamed his face as if to make sure that he understood. "Let's do it," he said, and his tone was decisive. She saw that he was stubborn and could not be dissuaded.

After hearing about the pros and cons of leaving Uganda and going back to India, she wasn't sure what to say to him. She knew that once he had made up his mind nothing would change it. She had never known him to reverse a decision, so she chose not to dispute the point.

The plan was made. Radha would go with the kids to India and Raj would follow after completion of his contract. Till that time, she would ensure school admission of both the kids.

"Maybe you're right," she said at last. She saw his expression changed from concern to compassion.

"Maybe?" he repeated.

Silence greeted his final thought.

16. Homeland

In need of Star point for
setting the Sail

It's never too late to push yourself out of your comfort zone, and it's never too late to dive into something bigger All it takes is desire, sincere effort, and a firm commitment to keep sailing against all odds.

*

After completing the remaining three months of contract with the organization in Uganda, the evening finally arrived for Raj to head back home.

He boarded the flight and a few moments of personal quietness fell upon him. Twenty minutes into the flight, he revisited everything that he had experienced, observed, and felt in Uganda.

His heart turned with eager longing for the home he had left four years back.

"My destination" he said with a happy smile shining across his face. The happiness was of a different kind. It was neither exciting nor overwhelming. It was serene and calm. It was the happiness that one gets after toiling for years, when patience and determination are rewarded in the end.

*

And there, before, and below him, was the beautiful Ahmedabad city that had just then come into view.

The long flight down to India gave Raj the opportunity to have some well-earned rest. On reflection, he had no more than a couple of periods of uninterrupted sleep since the previous day. It seemed like a lifetime had elapsed since then, but there was so much going on in his life at the present that he hardly had the time to catch his breath.

On his return the joy of the family in welcoming him back, and his own joy at finding himself again among them was immense. It was a good feeling. He now felt that he had things under control, despite the apparent chaos. For the first time, he could relax a bit and he and his family hoped this would become their normal lifestyle. He was so happy to be surrounded by loved ones. It was like a family reunion, and he felt an overwhelming sense of joy as well as a sense of long-overdue homecoming.

As the evening ended, the girls got ready for bed, while Radha helped the girls into their night clothes. Raj came in soon after, to say good night to his girls. He spent a little time playing with them. Before kissing them good night, he stuck his hand under the arms of his daughter's and tickled their ribs, making them thrash around in their bed while laughing and squealing for him to stop.

Their giggling was music to his ears. "Good night, my babies. Papa loves you!"

"Good night, Papa. Love you too." In the night discussion went on between Radha and Raj for future of their daughters. Both were confident and reaffirmed that despite these hard times in life, now they will work upon a stability again.

This day has gotten the best of him. Exhaustion tugged at his body. Then he turned out the light and closed his eyes amid his many thoughts.

His thoughts travelled on his work, and as he did, he thought about everything that happened. He could not wait too long for some real action.

He drifted off to sleep, confident that tomorrow would be a changing day in his life. He went to his room and laid in the comfort of his bed, staring at the ceiling thinking about all the things that needed to be done tomorrow.

*

It was a glorious Monday morning. The day was indeed beautiful. The sky was bright and brilliant blue. Shuffling out of the bedroom, he took in a deep breath, shutting his eyes against the early morning sun, letting the warm rays wash over him. When he opened his eyes, he saw deep, dark-brown eyes of his wife looking at him.

The distinctive aroma of ginger tea was in the air, and it reminded him that he was home. This was what he had missed the most. The fragrance of home, the taste of homemade tea, the laughter of his daughters, and most importantly, the concern of his wife and parents.

"Morning," he smiled to Radha as she walked in with a tray of tea and biscuits. "I'm glad you've come back home. Many things were missing when you were not here," she said with a warm smile. She held out the cup of tea. "Special tea for you." He took a sip and smacked his lips in satisfaction.

Just then the girls came running to him calling "Papa!" A beautiful smile spread across his face. He touched their heads and said, "Good morning." His eyes lingered fondly upon the beaming faces of his daughters. "My girls, getting ready for school?" He smiled at his daughters. Both the girls were Papa's girls. "Of course." They beamed. "I'm always ready for school," said his elder daughter. He laughed. "I am glad to hear that. Let's hope you keep that attitude all the way through college." She giggled. "I'll try Papa." Radha flashed him an impish smile, as she got up to prepare breakfast for the kids. She loved seeing him with the children.

Shortly, she walked out of the kitchen with two lunch boxes. Her long dark hair was pulled back into a ponytail. "You better go before you're late," she told their daughters, as they packed away the books in their bags. "Right, come on now, run." Grabbing the lunch boxes, the two girls planted a kiss on their mother's cheek, quickly turning away squealing while Radha shook her head in amusement. "The girls look so happy," whispered Radha.

After dropping the girls to school, during the drive back home, a realisation struck him that his little daughters were growing up fast. He had missed so many years of their lives, because of work, and suddenly they were going off to school. Soon they would be off to high school, he thought, then college, and then they'd be married and have children of their own. He didn't know why he cried, didn't know if it was joy or regret, but he couldn't stop the tears either way. Eventually, when he parked his car at home, he wiped his face and, with the smile of a loving father, entered his house.

*

Raj earnestly started investing sufficient time and energy in job-hunting. He spent several hours going over the day's job openings in the newspaper. For the first few months, he looked for a position like the one he'd just left, but he expanded his search when he was unable to find such an opening. Not long after, he successfully landed himself a job as a site in charge in a service company called Splendid Service Company (SSC). It was exciting time in the world of services.

Soon he headed a site in Sholapur. About forty machines were installed at the site and he took overall responsibility for stabilization of the entire site operations which involved maintenance of machines, health and safety, administration, human resource, accounts, and finance of the site. The team was formed, and operations of the site continued for 8-9 months.

Things were hectic for the next couple of months. He used to wonder how quickly months flew. Working late into the evenings was exciting for him, rather than a hindrance. He loved implementing new things – ideas, concepts, planning, and strategizing about how he would do it. Considering operations to be performed at height, safety risk assessment and mitigation was his prime focus.

After the site was stabilised, he was told to go to another site. Although he went to that site, but simultaneously he looked for other openings within SSC. He came across an opening in the Marketing department of the company in Ahmedabad location, his hometown.

*

Raj was happy! The employment opportunity in his hometown was the best job he could imagine. From now on, he thought to himself, he could live in peace in his hometown, among his own people. He could spend more time with his parents, little daughters, and his wife.

However, he soon realised that there was hardly any contribution in marketing since there were so many people in the department. He expressed his concern to his boss who told to work on developing a market in SEZ in Kutch, Gujarat.

He was given a new project to work on. The project involved conceptualisation and entire study of the regulations of industry. It was a challenge and Raj really enjoyed it. He loved learning new concepts about his industry and loved seeing the results. Along his journey, Raj realized that he needed help. He met a person that became a pivotal influence in his career, Mr. Arjun. The gentleman, who was heading the regulatory team of the State, explained various new concepts and regulations available. Raj was always good with concepts, so understanding the complex regulations came easily to him.

Raj always believed in walking on a path of continual learning, and he loved any opportunity to find techniques that could change, improve, and advance. He recalled the words of his father that the challenges in a job were like a puzzle, some can be simple, and some take a lot of time and patience, but each one brings a sense of satisfaction.

As someone who was a believer of the holistic domain; Raj created a well-structured and professional presentation that incorporated the viability, sustainability, bottlenecks in the regulations, along with recommendations. This was highly well received by the office in Mumbai and his efforts were applauded.

But soon, the company begun downsizing the marketing team across the entire country operations. Many marketing professionals in the company worried that their jobs were in jeopardy. Raj too was worried over the probability of losing his job. However, his boss assured him that he would accommodate Raj somehow in Ahmedabad.

However, Raj didn't like the sound of that. He didn't want any concession. He had confidence in himself and confidence in his abilities, and faith that things would turn out all right. Although, he was humbled at the proposition offered, he politely declined the favour offered to him.

He debated all his options and finally settled for a transfer to some other work site.

New location, new challenges and strangely, he relished that thought.

17. Challenging Decision

Adjusting the Sail

Raj wrestled his eyes open to find he was in a completely unfamiliar territory. He stared at the white walls and high ceiling of the room; the fresh smell of the blanket clenched in his hands only added more confusion. Cupping one hand to shade his eyes, he blinked at the walls- and wondered what the hell he was doing there.

*

And then he remembered. It was a hotel room! He'd checked in the night before. He had moved to Kolhapur and temporarily checked into a hotel there for 15 days, till the time he found an accommodation in the city. He had requested a transfer to another location in the country, after being in various locations in same company in these last 2 years of coming back to India. and he received an opportunity to work in Kolhapur in the Business Development Department of Splendid Service Company (SSC).

Very soon, he adjusted to a new profile, new working environment, new skills and responsibilities.

A new beginning has commenced.

Raj was busy. He felt passionate about his work and loved operating on overdrive. His pioneering spirit loved new challenges.

As soon as he started work in Kolhapur, he began planning and implementing holistic strategies on how to make the organisation more customer driven. He gave a lot of thought to the customer service issues that needed to be fixed. Raj realised that the longstanding customer relationships were at risk. The bigger issue was the opportunity cost. The unhappy customers took too much of his team's time. As a result, they distracted the team from the larger task at hand. He just wanted operations to be streamlined without any bottlenecks.

A database was created, each customer categorised based on issues, and using that information, the team created a customer relationship plan, outlining specific action steps to resolve issues.

In all of them, Raj stood by his team's side, giving the team prominence, because he knew that without their efforts nothing could be accomplished, may be his heart has seen the Diwali Anar success every Diwali. Or maybe it was the experience of holistic thinking that gave Raj his people skills. He was well liked and was an expert at motivating his team. This was not because he knew that he needed them to succeed, but because he was genuinely interested in their success.

Raj knew he needed a catalyst for change, and this project had been a springboard for action. One thing was clear: To get to that next level of performance, to be more effective, change had to come from within. The group had some of the brightest minds in the company. He was confident that this was possible, and he knew with the right level of support, he could get the job done.

*

It was a marvellous night, soft and still. His eyes gazed upon the sky above. There was no moon, and overhead the sky was ablaze with the millions of twinkling stars. There was a strange absence of something, an absentness that he felt in everything. Everything was fine at work, but the claws of dissatisfaction kept scratching at his spirit. He was filled with dismay about some missing element in his current profile. He wondered if-despite his rich experience-was he successful?

Over the course of several weeks, Raj found himself going into a full-scale re-examination of where he was with his career and life and what he had accomplished.

*

With a deep thought, he looked at the watch. It was 8.30 pm. He decided to take a hot shower, he thought over and over and over, why not ask Radha if she would join him to Kolhapur, for the entire duration of his job. His mind was made up. Once he decided, he rarely questioned his own decision.

He hurried out of the shower and spent a few minutes going over what he was going to say to Radha, and just how he was going to say it. This was going to be difficult for Raj.

He dialled the phone. The phone on the other end rang. Radha had just returned home from her clinic, when the phone rang. She was surprised to hear from Raj so late in the evening, and she asked, "Is everything all right?" Her voice was low and suspicious. The complete silence on the other end of the phone caught her immediate attention.

"What? What happened, Raj? Are you okay?" She held the phone tightly and spoke with a frightened, out-of-breath voice. Again, silence greeted her question.

A moment before she heard his voice, she felt a feeling of dread. "Yes, everything is all right," Raj replied.

"Are you sure?" she asked anxiously. "You sound upset." She could hear him exhale in a very deep breath.

"It's just a slight problem at the office, that's all." Radha knew he had something disturbing on his mind.

"What is it, Raj?" she asked gently. Life had taught her to stay gentle despite huge turmoil inside.

"I was thinking that—" he paused.

"Thinking what?"

"Listen Radha, I've got an idea. And don't say 'no' without thinking about it—OK?" he muttered, trying to clear the tension building in his vocal cords.

She waited. Confusion crossed her brow.

"Well-I want that you-you should join me here in Kolhapur next week!" said Raj excitedly.

He felt her reaction was a surprise and that she was about to answer. Fearing a 'no' he went on, "Pack up and you and Mitu come here."

Radha was taken aback; she didn't know what to say. "Now, just a minute…" Radha began. "Join you?" she said in a slow disturbed voice, "In Kolhapur?"

"No, you're joking!" Radha said as she took a deep breath.

"I'm dead serious," he said in an offended tone.

"-no-I don't think-"They both were silent for a few confusing seconds.

The relocation to Kolhapur would mean uprooting the family once again where Raj had been already moving in the last 2 years and Radha had somehow balanced work with life with young one with her and older one in boarding school and moving away from their extended family and friends, not to mention leaving her career again and the children having to change schools. The change would impact Mitu more than her older sibling, who was already studying in a boarding school. Mitu was pre-school age, and it meant uprooting her and taking her some place entirely new and different.

"I don't-" Radha said, then paused again, and said, "What about Mitu's school? Uprooting her for a new city, new school, new friends…." Raj detected a note of reluctance in her voice in uprooting the kid's school.

"Don't worry." He said, interrupting her. "Just be patient. It will be taken care of. She's only in grade two! She will go to the best school here." Anushka is already in such a good boarding school and happily enjoying and exceling in all fields, Raj's voice was astonishingly deep and calm.

Radha listened in stunned silence. "And-and my clinic?" she asked vaguely, as if struggling to understand him. "What about my job with SAC?"

Raj was silent for a while, and then he said slowly as he scrubbed his jaw. "You should probably wind it up."

"But Raj…" He stopped her from saying more. "Can you do this for me?"

"Well…." she wasn't sure what to say.

*

"Tell me," he said, in a low, grave voice. "I have been wondering lately…...Do you think I have failed professionally?" It was a painful question, and quickly Raj swallowed down. He anguished over the thought even as he expressed it.

Radha was in shock, listening to this question and wisely regained her composure and said, "No way, Raj!" Her voice was strained, "I know things haven't been that great lately. But you've still survived, not failed." He took a deep breath and let it out slowly. Coming from his wife, the words uttered by her, and the meaning behind them, were reassuring and touching to Raj.

"But tell me, what makes you think so, Raj?" asked Radha, in a voice as calm as he could assume.

"Because I feel that people must definitely be thinking that way…." He trailed off dryly. He turned silent for another minute, and then, instead of a direct answer, he put a question in a gloomy way: "Do you also think I am an aimless wanderer professionally?" Even before Radha could reply, he continued. "You know," he said, "-I have wandered directionless, from this job to that to that. I have no position to show for all my expertise and experience." His voice carried a tone of intensity that Radha hadn't heard before.

"Raj, you have always carried out roles and responsibilities effectively, honestly and diligently with all accountabilities, in all the industries that you've worked. In fact, you took calls of going to Nigeria, then to Uganda and eventually back to India and changed places in India as per your plan. You chose and did what you planned what can be better. You cannot reach to Delhi by buying ticket of Jaipur. If you do your job well, then whatever failures occur are not your fault." replied Radha, choosing her words carefully.

"I don't know," Raj said with a sad sigh, "I feel that everyone is dismissive about the importance of work. I guess that in the world of corporate game players, professional manipulation is a norm." said Raj. "It's a different world out there." He sighed. "Perhaps I was too ambitious for them….," he murmured in a sad undertone, "or maybe I was a misfit…."

"They're all blinded," Radha reminded him gently. "They can't see the elephant. You cannot let blind men define your elephant. So do not consider yourself as a failure or a misfit. You understand what I am saying?" Raj nodded his head and agreed: "You're right, I understand what you mean."

She managed to keep a note of firmness in her tone.

"Don't stress yourself too much. I think you should sleep now. You sound very tired." She added.

Raj conceded…Radha was right. He did need sleep. He flopped down on the bed. He meant to sleep but rest didn't come. Grimly he turned onto his side, spending the next hour or so pondering over the environment at work that offered little outlet for his entrepreneurial talent.

With his mind thus agitated, his thoughts were directed to Radha. He knew she was the only person who would support him, no matter what he decided. She had always graciously allowed him to have the final decision.

One thing was for certain. He would insist on having Radha move to Kolhapur. Even if it meant letting her clinic go.

This decision to relocate to Kolhapur obviously meant a lot to him. To both. And to his daughters.

The self-introspection continued.

Today, he was everything he never thought he would be focussed, determined, and hardworking. It was a core belief, unknown and buried deeply within him, that the application of holistic thinking was the key to success. He now understood that it was so important to plan your life and not drift wherever the wind blows. Now a sense of purpose had entered his life.

*

The last two days before the relocation to Kolhapur were hectic and painful as it was done in just 5 days. Resigning from job, getting TC from school, making Mitu understand, helping parents and to pack with her own heart and mind talking frantically whole time about this decision. Radha packed up box after box and lined them in the living room. And amid the frantic packing, the day of the actual move from Ahmedabad arrived.

For Raj, the actual move was just the beginning involving in relocating his family; finding a good accommodation, and most importantly, getting Mitu enrolled in a good school.

After securing Mitu's admission in one of the best schools in Kolhapur, Raj rented an accommodation close to office and the family moved in there. After spending a few days setting up the new house together, the family started getting accustomed to the new ways. Soon they had comfortably settled down.

*

"Raj, are you okay?" Radha asked, as she entered the bedroom.

He was sitting up, leaning against several pillows and tapping his forehead with a half frown upon his face. Radha could tell he was absorbed in deep contemplation. "What are you thinking about?" she asked him.

He paused. "About Mitu's admission…."

She asked with a puzzled expression. "That's already been

117

taken care of, isn't it?"

Looking thoughtfully across the floor, Raj answered slowly, "Yes. It is."

"Then what about it?" She opened her eyes in surprise.

She had asked a simple question. But fifteen minutes passed, and Raj had still not answered the question. He was caught in memories, sitting in what looked like a trance.

When he looked up, his eyes had a mournful expression, and he said, "I need some time to be alone. I don't know how to explain it, I'll talk more to you about this later." She blinked back in disbelief, then sighed. "Okay," she said and left. Her heart flipped in fear, now what was to come.

As he lay on the bed, staring at the ceiling, many thoughts flooded his mind.

There was a harsh introspection, accompanied by self-criticism. It was about something that had never bothered him before, but now it did- financial security.

"What have you earned in all these years, Raj," a voice in his head told him. "You had to think twice for your daughter's admission fee!" It was a nightmare, one he'd never even considered, come true. He glanced down at his hands, the coarse hands of a man who had never bothered with accumulating money or saved anything worthwhile.

His mind loomed over his minimal personal cash flow. He shook his head ever so slightly, clearly disappointed. Until this day, money never mattered to him. He always felt that had more than enough for his own wants, which were moderate in the extreme. But the big figure in the check given for Mitu's school admission was an eye-opener. He simply found it unbearable to think of his child having to settle for just fine and was so angry with himself for bringing his family in such a situation. He had everything in Uganda. A chauffeur driven car, a furnished home, 24X7 maid, Radha working in a hospital, Children in good school. How he wished he could turn back the clock and rearrange everything about his family.

Raj had been raised in a family that valued academic success. From the very beginning, he too had no worries or no concerns about the fact that he had no big money in his kitty. He'd never been bothered about owning a fancy car, having the best apartment or wearing branded clothes. After marriage too, Radha had adjusted very well.

But suddenly, he could not stop himself from feeling that he should have put in more planning in the financial security of his daughters in order to keep his head above water.

What a mess, he kept telling himself, and the eternal question kept popping up in his mind, how did it all happen?

He wanted to blame someone, but he knew there was no one to blame but himself. That self-loathing killed him. His anger turned on himself.

*

It was already after seven, and darkness had draped the room now. Radha walked in and switched on the lights of the bedroom. She looked at him wide-eyed and asked, "What is wrong with you? You've been sitting here for over three hours; do you know that?" She sounded worried.

He waited a bit before speaking. "Radha." He made an effort to sit up and rested his dark, unspeakably moist eyes on her face. "I forgot something?" he remarked. His brown eyes shone with worry, a frown wrinkling his brow.

She raised an eyebrow. "Really? What is it?" Radha looked at him, confusion crossing her features as she tried to anticipate his thoughts.

He didn't speak, and after a few moments, with a down-turned smile of deep contemplation, he nodded abstractly as if agreeing with some inner voice. "Radha-," he started to say, without taking his eyes off her for a second, "I know what I forgot," His lips quivered.

She returned the question. "What?". Now more worried and scared.

"About what, Raj?" There was no answer. His eyes stared straight into hers, and for a moment she thought he was trying to hold back tears. His gaze dropped in surrender, "Uh, it's hard to explain— I forgot to plan for my family." She gasped, startled by his words. "Plan!"

He nodded apprehensively. "I was selfish, Radha, "he said matter-of-fact. "I thought-I believed-I knew what I wanted. And I damn near lost my mind-," he swallowed a couple of times and finished what he started to say, "-over my professional success." Raj visibly trembled as he spoke.

He rubbed his chin as he said in a lowered voice. "I'm saying that you don't deserve a man like me." Hot tears burned his eyes. As much as she wanted to, Radha couldn't argue. "I had been far too preoccupied in the pursuing my professional goals that I did not fulfil my family responsibilities. It never occurred to me that I-,"The expression in his eyes gave away the pain he felt inside.

"Raj-," Radha started to say. There was pain in her voice. "Has it ever occurred to you that, perhaps you missed out on some critical elements of the elephant?"

He stared at her and frowned,"What…"

Seeing him raise his eyebrows questioningly, she simply nodded and said, "Based on the parable of the blind men and the elephant, you put all sincere efforts in your work. You invested all your time and energy in your profession, because you were determined to excel." She paused and glanced at Raj to see that he was listening to her very intently.

Her voice took on a compassionate tone. "You blinded yourself to an important part of the elephant, which is your wife and children."

Radha continued in a soft but determined tone, you understood the Parable of blind men and the elephant very well but perhaps you missed the important part of family, health, social ties, and spiritual values in defining your elephant and hence feels these emotions.

"Your elephant was only your professional goals. In your dedication to your job, you were missing to the other elements that make your elephant complete." Radha looked away sadly and sighed. "I think that the missing element that you need to reflect on, and address is your family, health, social ties and your spiritual values; all these are critical pieces of the elephant."

For several minutes after Radha stopped speaking, Raj squeezed his eyes shut in deep thinking. Anushka was in 10th now and Mitu in 3rd std.

Finally, he stood, sighed deeply, and shook his head as if clearing his thoughts. "Yes -" he said, with tenderness in his eyes. "You are correct."

*

An incident that could have ruined Raj's mental health became an excellent opportunity for his self-realization.

Now he realized what he should have been doing-taking care of his wife and daughters.

And another thing he'd realized was there was no use in looking back. But he was glad to have Radha as his partner who was strong, wise and had taken good care of children and supported him despite suffering herself and never complaining during these hardships.

18. A Complete Elephant

All set to Sail for Freedom

"The journey of a thousand miles begins with one step."

Raj had now taken that first important step which represented a big step forward. And with this step, the future of his career looked extremely promising, and with it an even bigger opportunity to enrich the life of his loved ones, now smiled at him.

*

Raj's position at the company shifted over the years. An opportunity soon opened in the organisation for Service Head. Raj was appointed for the position, and he was transferred to the main office of the company located at Pune. The profile involved taking care of customers at Pune, Aurangabad, Nagpur, Ahmednagar, Kolhapur, and Goa. It was a huge responsibility and the new role called for a relocation to Pune.

Decision-making was hard. But a heightened sense of clarity had come in his brain now; one that he hadn't felt in a long time. Planning at professional level had always been his strongest card in the deck, but he had never fully realized its power in personal relationships until now.

After a lot of deliberations and considerations on the implications and discussions with Radha, his mind was made up.

"Another rushed relocation? More rushed than the last one?" asked Radha. The last thing she needed was an unscheduled change of place. She wondered what destiny now had in store for them.

"Well," he said, with an odd laugh. Raj shook his head. "You know…" and then stopped without completing the sentence.

She tried to read the pause that followed. "What?" she asked with a puzzled expression.

He took a deep breath and then slowly said, "Not anymore." He smiled and looked at her from beneath half-lowered eyelids. "Our final destination," he said calmly. "And you'll never regret it, trust me. I have defined my complete Elephant involving my professional and personal life."

Radha looked at him in disbelief, trying to comprehend what he was saying, or wanted to say.

*

Though, naturally, the relocation posed several problems, it had the advantage of allowing his mistakes of the past to be corrected. He did not want things to be completed in haste. It was an important matter and needed to be settled with patience. Raj had done the work; he had examined all his options and was ready to execute his planned strategy. He planned every detail of the move well in advance; what needed to be done and how to do it. He took a long time refining every detail and made another move to Pune.

This first step was a complete success. Yes, it did cost him quite a bit of money. But he could see that the upsides of this step were huge.

Professionally too, things started to show signs of improvement, but there were other things dominant in him now, far more urgent. Now the only thing that was important to him was to improve the quality of his daily life and carrying out some of his "family's forgotten dreams."

First and foremost, he wanted to erase all that his wife had experienced. He knew that he could not change the past but could alter the future. He loved her and knew the magnitude of sacrifices made by Radha. He was now utterly committed to ensuring the happiness of Radha, who had cared enough to stand by him.

He began doing the work towards becoming a better husband and a better parent. In short, this meant planning and prioritizing quality experiences with his family, that is, weekend getaways, dine out at the city's popular restaurants, movie nights, and holidays. In the long term, it meant providing a stable and secure future for his family. He shared a small and very close-knit group of likeminded friends with Radha who enriched his life and shared heart-to-heart-connections.

He took his family very seriously, especially his responsibilities as a father. He made sure that he attended his children's performances and school events with Radha when he could. He sat in the front seats of a school function, exuding pride as he watched his children perform. He instructed his daughters in the way of wisdom, specifically developing their character and skills for life and vocation. He believed that it was the main duty of a father to exercise a strong moral influence over both the girls and inculcate in them sound moral values and orderly conduct.

He participated in the execution of plans for the educational outcomes of his daughters.

His elder daughter, Anushka, studied in a boarding school at Coimbatore from eighth grade till tenth grade. She wanted to study medicine and become a doctor like her mother. She was always a topper in class, and an all-rounder, who always did well in all the tests. He-and Radha knew that this was a crucial period of her academic life, when she needed support and guidance of her parents. After lot of deliberation with his wife, they enrolled her in a prestigious school in Pune. To assist her in the preparation of various medical entrance examinations and competitive entrance exams, Radha enrolled her in preparatory classes.

Radha found strength in the staunch support of her husband, and they started working as a team for their children's future. Together, they tried to provide an enriching environment required for proper development for their children. They patiently communicated to find out what interested them, what they dreamt of. They provided continuous positive reinforcements as well as positive feedback for their academic accomplishments and development of their strengths. Since the younger daughter, Mitu, tested very high on musical abilities, they steered her to music and enrolled her in classical dance classes and other culturally related programs to blossom beautifully and completely.

He started to take his daughters to all the places they'd want to go, showered them constant love, attention and praise at every small act of achievement. They were very happy together, and Raj could see the biggest smiles he had seen in years. Raj used to tell her daughters "I have not given you chauffer driven car but I have been a chauffer in your car."

It was time for Raj to start living the life that he had always dreamt of; a life filled with laughter and good times with his family. A happy life that he and Radha had created together. Along with the professional hard work that he continued.

*

Soon Raj moved to another position of higher responsibility and started heading the State customer service division. He fit into this larger role with remarkable ease. He felt like he was discovering new leadership strengths and passions. Using the well-honed skills of his profession, he built healthy relationships with stakeholders.

In conformity with a new job description, Raj prioritized teamwork and talent development. He developed inter-personal relationship with his team members.

He instructed his team to inculcate holistic thinking in their individual scope of work. He made sure to align the vision of his team with the organisation's mission and goals.

In his efforts to inculcate holistic thinking in his team, he started to share the "pearls of wisdom" that he once gained from his mentors. He often shared stories and personal situations on how he had applied holistic thinking in his life situations. The team loved to hear holistic principles and its applications.

"To be successful you first have to know how to look at the bigger picture," he often stated to his team during training sessions.

"Sir, why do you always use the elephant parable in your conversation when we come to you for a solution to a problem?" a member of his team smiled slightly and asked during one of the training sessions.

"Team," he began, "there's a simple explanation."

"In the context of the elephant story, we learn that things

should be set as a whole and not by a single target. Each blind man walked away confident that he knew what an elephant was like." He paused for a moment to rest, then continued. "We're like these blind men. We tend to view a problem through a narrow frame. What we need to do is conceptualize our problems on a broader stage. We need to use our imagination to broaden our outlook by looking aggressively at the bigger picture." Raj paused once again and glanced around the group. He saw his team listening intently to this intriguing philosophy.

A large smile transformed the face of his team member, as he said, "I think I understand what you're saying about the importance of the elephant. When we come to you with a problem, you ask us different questions about the bottlenecks. Now I know why-you're trying to make sure that I look at a problem from several viewpoints, aren't you? I have understood the concept of Elephant which needs to be applied in all aspects of Life."

Raj looked around him at the assembled team. He was pleased to notice that all of them were soaking up everything he said.

He smiled and his eyes twinkled as he looked over his spectacles at the faces of the boys in front of him. "Just like the soft, subdued rays from the sun bring balance to surroundings, similarly holistic thinking brings a dynamic balance between inner and outer environments It helps us become better at setting and achieving goals."

That concluding line met with a round of applause, which echoed throughout the office.

A warm pride and satisfaction in his expression echoed louder in his heart than the applause of the crowd. Raj was finally happy to be where he felt he belonged, in the spotlight sharing his knowledge of holistic thinking.

19. Freedom

My Sailboat- My Life
- My Rule

Raj ultimately moved into Strategic Business Planning department and started to be looked upon as an expert in customer centricity. He led assessments of various organisations on Performance driven work culture.

He drew up a mentoring programme that fitted the company culture and answered the needs of accelerated revenue and customer satisfaction. Raj was much sought for mentoring projects. He mentored many students from IITs, IIMs, even students from Canada.

He initiated webinar, to develop a seamless method to implement new Government regulation which required overcoming challenges of customer resistance and achieving customer satisfaction. The program provided an outlook of the relevant issues and solutions to allow higher service levels. Over hundred people attended the webinar, which included employees from various departments. The program was a key milestone in the process of training future generations in the organisation.

*

Raj entered the training room where a bunch of fresh university graduates who had entered the energy workforce, waited for him. The training program was designed to adequately prepare new joiners to be entry-level wind turbine service technicians.

Once all the participants settled themselves, Raj started the training session with a question, "I'd like to start today's session by first asking you a question. How many of you feel that you are SUCCESSFUL?"

The room was completely silent. No one volunteered. Some of the participants shook their heads.

Raj smiled and looked around the room. "No one has achieved anything till date!"

"Well, let me rephrase my question. In college, how many of you have achieved a score you desperately wanted?" The tone of Raj's voice didn't convey an inquiry, it was a challenge.

Several hands immediately went up.

He pointed to one of the participants and asked him to highlight his scores to everyone.

The participant said, "In college, I set my target to securing a minimum of 60% in the exam. I was able to beat my target and secured 70%."

Raj applauded and said, "Very good. That's a wonderful achievement, isn't it?"

"And what did you do to reach that goal?"

The participant breathed in, still debating, and then spoke softly. "I made a timetable covering all the topics. Also, I referred to the previous year's question papers. I also participated in group studies."

"Great," said Raj. "So, what he did was that he visualised what he wanted, made a roadmap, or a plan, that laid out what he wanted, what he needed to do, and a timetable of daily targets to get it, am I right?" The participant nodded as if the power of words was dawning on him for the first time. The other participants also nodded their heads in agreement after Raj's explanation.

"Anyone else has achieved something?" After a moment of quiet think time, another participant quickly raised his hand.

"Yes... You please." The participant stood up, and he too gave an example which he considered an achievement in his engineering results. After applauding him, Raj said, "Now, you have heard two of the achievements of your colleagues. Both planned a target and achieved it."

"That's what is SUCCESS...Planning to accomplish your targets."

Raj paused briefly to let his training sink into the participants and then continued, "When you get good grades in school, it means you are successful. When you get admission in a specific college, that's success. When you complete an assignment, that's success!"

"He," said Raj, pointing at the student, "did his best and scored higher in his academic scores than the target he had set for himself. Although he may not be a topper, but he was successful! Why? Because he defined his own success. Because there was self-satisfaction in the result he got."

The participants recognised that this was different from any ordinary lecture. They were totally captivated by the learning concepts.

"I always thought," a small voice said from the back of the

room, "that I was a failure because I did not get good academic grades."

"Well, sadly enough, I thought so too at one point of time," said Raj with a smile on his face. I used to be a happy-go-lucky boy, least interested in getting good grades. I was always scolded by my parents to score well. But I never listened to them." The participants erupted in an enthusiastic laughter.

"To be successful in life -- for any endeavour – STRIVE to give your best, have the clear VISION of what you want, and ACHIEVE it."

Once you make the decision to strive, visualise and achieve, you set sail on an incredible journey. There will be waves of challenges, but the focus and the desire to achieve, provides the freedom to move forward towards the destination you have chosen for yourself.

The class sat still, looking intently upon their mentor, waiting for some more words, he paused and left with one remark, "Be Ready to break free and discover your calling."

With that, Raj walked out of the room, smiling brightly.

*

After few years, Raj walked into the training room, where the batch was waiting for the training to begin.

The room had a welcoming atmosphere. A projector hung from the ceiling and there was a screen before the projector to display the slides and the videos of the presentation. A desk and large whiteboard stood at one corner. Seven big round tables were neatly arranged that seated seven to eight persons each.

The room had diverse participants from all departments – engineering, supply chain management, projects, admin, finance, HR, IT, sales, and safety. Raj strode in and all eyes were turned towards him.

"Silo" mentality was a concern in the organisation. All departments 'operated in silos,' meaning they weren't acting cohesively, and Raj was determined to implement a more collaborative work system that included teamwork. He understood that silo syndrome could derail the progress of the organisation. To deal with the potential negative impact of this mentality, Raj designed a training program.

Casting a swift glance around the room, he expressed a warm welcome to all participants.

After a fun-filled ice breaker that was designed to put everyone at ease, he said, "Let's start with this," and he switched on the projector to play a video address by the CEO.

The video began with a reinforcement of the organisation's vision of "Being the best service industry in the sector." The CEO then conveyed that there were two areas that created a competitive disadvantage for the organisation in achievement of this vision. The first area was a "silo" mind-set, employees focussed on department goals instead of organisational goals, with each department operating on its own, and second area was the follow-up culture wherein lot of follow ups were required within various teams and members to get certain activity executed. Stressing the importance of cross-departmental collaboration, the CEO closed the speech urging people at all levels-from new associates to top executives-to align together to create a winning culture of collaboration in the organisation.

After hearing the video, most employee showed a puzzled expression on their faces. "No, no, that's not true, we do not have the silo mentality!" said a participant, while a few others nodded their heads to endorse the views expressed by him. Others, by their lack of participation, were likely feeling the same, but they were not as vocal.

The air seemed to be imbued with uncertainty and anxiety, in which Raj stood like a red beacon of hope to clear this confusion. "You all seem to be a little anxious after hearing the message of our CEO, isn't it?" The participants were unanimous in answering affirmatively.

"You want a way out of the confusion? Let me start with a question."

He then asked, "What do you think is the most important part of an organisation?"

After a designated period of discussion with peers sitting on the table, Raj asked for a representative from each table to present their answer. Everyone mentioned that sales and after-sales service were the most important departments. The next few minutes were conducted as an interactive discussion which elicited information from participants on why they believed that sales department was the life of any firm.

"We have been in this room for a little over two hours now, and everyone looks little tired. So why don't we take a ten-minute tea break, and then we will continue." Raj said with a smile.

When he resumed the session after the break, he requested all participants to arrange themselves in groups or clusters according to their respective departments. All employees without exception responded favourably and enthusiastically to the unique format of the session.

"So, now let's build on the response of everyone in the room. Before the break, we all agreed that since the sales department set the direction for the company's products and services and dealt with the customers, it was of prime importance."

All nodded in agreement.

He took of his glasses and cleaned them with his handkerchief. "Now let me ask you another question. Where do you visualise yourself in five years from now? I want you to take a moment and think about it."

A nervous silence set in. All participants looked back at him with no response. They seemed surprised, for the question sounded irrelevant to the training. After a while, answers emerged from several tables and most of the responses fell into the category of becoming an entrepreneur. A few employees from IT department stated that they wanted to be computer programmers and develop a mobile based application. An employee from finance stated that he wanted to be a consultant in a huge firm. Another expressed a desire of being an owner of a manufacturing unit of refurbished motorcycles.

"Okay, let's use this example of setting a bike service unit as our guide for a moment and do some brainstorming," Raj said.

He waited for a moment and then said in a clear, loud voice. "What do you think should be the Unique Selling Proposition (USP) of the unit, that the entrepreneur should ensure?

The engineering guys said that the design of bikes will be the USP. On the other hand, the operations people said service quality will be USP. The HR folks made the case that since a company is made up of people, without having quality operators, nothing else could happen. So, it was their department that would ultimately determine the success of the unit. He paused before he spoke again. The supply chain department claimed that the engineering and operations department could do nothing unless the supply chain supported them. Similarly, the finance department viewed themselves as the keepers of the money in the firm, so the success would rest in their hands.

The admin department contended that since the department ensures the comfort, and healthy indoor environment, it was of prime importance.

Raj intervened. Do you all remember the parable of five blind man and an Elephant. Everybody was aware of it. He continued "In the session before tea, you all said that sales and marketing is the most important department. But now you are just like blind men, talking about each of your department being most important!" The class was silent.

He pulled up a chair and sat down. "So, what do you conclude?" Raj asked.

No one spoke.

Raj responded. "See for each group their department is most important, without understanding that all departments are complimentary to each other for the success of the complete unit. We are acting like blind men without knowing the complete elephant, this is Silo mentality. Working in a silo might feel like you're doing nothing wrong-after all, you're dedicating all your working hours to your department and your team members, right? Maybe not. What is happening is that each of your department or "silo" is operating as a separate unit with an independent budget, management, goal, and objective. What this is leading to is the silo syndrome, where each of your department is rarely collaborating with those departments on the outside of your established silos."

The truth is that each department contributes to the whole. The engineering team designs the product, sales bring the customers, operations service the product bought by consumers and customer service ensures customer satisfaction. So, it is important to remove those silos that each of your department have within you. And when you do this, it ensures that you build more trusting relationship, boost team spirit, and ensures success. And its ripple effect on the organisation is that the vision is accomplished, which is what our CEO just mentioned in the video. Now here, let us apply the parable, let us not become those blind man looking at individual department goals. Because then you will be blinded by the partial perspective and not able to comprehend the whole, organisational goals.

Raj continued with intensity to make his point. He said "Similarly in our personal life every member of family, be it father, mother, son, daughter, grandparent, grandchildren, wife, husband, daughter in law, mother-in-law, friend …. whatever role we are performing we have freedom to grow, enrich ourselves by learning about other member(s) of family, their role and respect the interconnectedness of each other. We have mental silos there also. Let us overcome these silos and use our freedom to strive, visualise and achieve in all our roles."

All employees were silent, absorbing the concept and perception of wholeness at professional and personal levels.

The results of the training were impressive. All participants left the room with a much greater awareness of the mental silos that were getting in their way and slowing down the collective success of the organisation.

The workshop outcome was positive. It opened collaborative communication among employees, which resulted in greater enthusiasm for their jobs and hence greater productivity for the company. It allowed employees to experience job enrichment. They felt more intrinsically motivated towards their work. More importantly, it allowed employees to gain more insights into the various processes of the company and made them more sensitive to the contributions of other departments.

Most impressive, however, was the fact that it built an organisational culture that was built on freedom! Freedom to Grow. Yes, freedom - to think beyond their own sphere of work, respecting interconnectedness of the organization.

Everyone realised that their Freedom lies in defining clear goals, removing the shackles of myopia, self-doubts, apprehension, which acts like an Anchor and affect the growth.

*

Raj basked in peace, and it was of a different kind. It was neither exciting nor overwhelming. It was soothing like a prayer. It was serene and calm. It was the kind of happiness that one gets after toiling for years, when patience and determination are rewarded in due time.

The serenity spread itself, reaching and touching everyone who met him. The previous years had been difficult. There had been many emotional upheavals and lows, but then, he had fought those delicate moments.

Now, after a long time, Raj felt as one feels in a beautiful place where thoughts stop for a while, where fears rest, where worries do not bother anymore. He felt relieved.

It was an amazing feeling of freedom that he had always been craving, and he loved this freedom!

20. The Retirement Speech (Continued)

Sail is Set

The applause brought Raj back to the place where people had gathered for his retirement party.

Raj continued, "Freedom to me means "SVARAJ", our own Rule. It can be considered for both our own laws and our own regimes. The simple explanation is, we are all Humans; the only species who have their own mind. We can be free of inhibitions, self-doubts, worries, greed, rage, and impulsiveness. For this we need to define the Elephant of our life. We have the Freedom to choose our action plan. Setting them as our Rules to Strive, Visualise and Achieve our Elephant. The Clarity of the Elephant of our life with the Rules we set, gives us the Freedom of leading a joyful life. This is very empowering.

In college, everyone knew me as a carefree person who loved to laugh. I always believed "Life is simple, we complicate it with our own Mind."

When I entered the corporate world, the initial impression was not exciting. I didn't find any meaning in my daily work. There was a lack of meaningful contribution to the organisation! I got my Guru Mantra from my first mentor, Mr. Ram when he related professional life with the anecdote of five blind men and an elephant. An entirely new perspective unfolded before my eyes. That the organisation was a complete elephant, and we contribute to a part of it. If we see the whole elephant, we can contribute more.

Many a times in work, we experience that various things are done at the same time, there are too many people involved, and the work is being done in many different directions. "The problem is that we all work on the project like blind men. We destroy our possibility for coherence in the project, because none of us try to have complete picture of this elephant."

A holistic approach is what everyone should have in life, where our focus should not be on only mastering one part of the elephant. We should learn how this part completes the whole elephant The elephant must be visualised in each stage of work- the role, the design, with respect to whole organisation.

When I had not defined my elephant, my professional part had troubled me so much that I considered myself as a failure. I recollect telling Radha that "I have been wondering if I have failed, and that I am an aimless wanderer. Radha's reassuring words were "Raj, you have aways carried out roles and responsibilities effectively, honestly, and diligently with all accountabilities, in all the industries that you've worked. I realised, I had chosen all decisions in my work area and had followed them as per my plan. But still people were dismissive about the importance of my work and that in the world of corporate game players, professional manipulation is a norm. Radha had reminded me. "They cannot see your elephant. You cannot let blind men define your elephant. So do not consider yourself as a failure or a misfit". Radha had also brought out an important point that I had understood the Parable of blind men and the elephant very well but missed out the important part of my family, health, social ties, and spiritual values in defining my elephant and hence felt these emotions.

This was an excellent opportunity for me for self-realization. I am glad to have Radha as my partner who is strong, wise and have taken good care of children, parents and supported me. She compromised her medical career and never complained during these hardships.

I was then utterly committed to ensuring the happiness of Radha, who had cared enough about the family. I defined my Elephant. Worked towards becoming a better husband, better parent, and a better son. I used to tell my daughters "I have not given you chauffer driven car, but I have been a chauffeur in your car." I am proud to say that both of my daughters, Anushka and Mitu are pursuing Medicine, the forte of Radha. Both have got exposure in sports, dance, music, and they are also exposed to spirituality and moral values. I have shared a pearl of wisdom on Finance with my daughters that I got from my father "Never convert your Assets into an Expense". I share a small and very close-knit group of likeminded friends with Radha who have enriched my life and shared heart-to-heart-connections.

Moving forward to a new chapter, I commit myself to successfully mould this second half of my Life, with well-defined Elephant with My Rules for my Freedom."

That concluding line met with a round of applause, which echoed throughout the room, louder in Raj's Heart.

www.ingramcontent.com/pod-product-compliance
Lightning Source LLC
Chambersburg PA
CBHW041203150726
48006CB00016B/2101